The Subversive Copy Editor

Chicago Guides
to *Writing*, Editing*,*
and Publishing

THE SUBVERSIVE COPY EDITOR

ADVICE FROM CHICAGO

(or, How to Negotiate Good
Relationships with Your Writers,
Your Colleagues, and Yourself)

SECOND EDITION

Carol Fisher Saller

The University of Chicago Press
Chicago and London

Carol Saller is editor of the *Chicago Manual of Style Online*'s Q&A and writes the Editor's Corner for the *Chicago Manual of Style*'s *Shop Talk* blog. She occasionally writes about language and writing in academe for *Lingua Franca* at the *Chronicle of Higher Education* and is the author of several books for children, most recently the young adult novel *Eddie's War*.

The University of Chicago Press, Chicago 60637
The University of Chicago Press, Ltd., London
© 2009, 2016 by Carol Fisher Saller
All rights reserved. Published 2016.
Printed in the United States of America

25 24 23 22 21 20 19   3 4 5

ISBN-13: 978-0-226-23990-3 (cloth)
ISBN-13: 978-0-226-24007-7 (paper)
ISBN-13: 978-0-226-24010-7 (e-book)
DOI: 10.7208/chicago/9780226240107.001.0001

Library of Congress Cataloging-in-Publication Data

Names: Saller, Carol, author.
Title: The subversive copy editor: advice from
   Chicago (or, how to negotiate good relationships
   with your writers, your colleagues, and yourself) /
   Carol Fisher Saller.
Other titles: Chicago guides to writing, editing, and
   publishing.
Description: Second edition. | Chicago; London:
   University of Chicago Press, 2016. | © 2016 |
   Series: Chicago guides to writing, editing, and
   publishing | Includes bibliographical references
   and index.
Identifiers: LCCN 2015039591 | ISBN 9780226239903
   (cloth: alkaline paper) | ISBN 9780226240077
   (paperback: alkaline paper) | ISBN 9780226240107
   (e-book)
Subjects: LCSH: Copy editing.
Classification: LCC PN4784.C75 S25 2016 | DDC
   070.4/15—dc23 LC record available at http://lccn
   .loc.gov/2015039591

♾ This paper meets the requirements of ANSI/NISO
Z39.48-1992 (Permanence of Paper).

No passion in the world is equal to the
passion to alter someone else's draft.

H. G. WELLS

Contents

Preface to the Second Edition

While writing this book for the first time, I had no intention of hastening the book's obsolescence. I took care not to write in detailed ways about technology or publishing practices that would soon become dated. Seven years on, however, much in the first edition is out of step with current practices, and I hope this revision will remedy that.

Almost immediately after the book appeared in 2009, I started thinking of important things that I'd forgotten to say. So I created *The Subversive Copy Editor* blog, and for more than two years I posted tips and rants that I hoped would be of interest to writers and copy editors. For part of another year, I wrote for the *Chronicle of Higher Education* at the *Lingua Franca* blog with writing and publishing advice for students and scholars. Much of the material new to this edition is taken from or expands upon those writings.

Two subjects I barely touched upon in the first edition inspired two new chapters this time around: chapter 5, on the dangers of allegiance to outdated grammar and style rules, and chapter 12, on how to stay current in the language and technology issues that are important to anyone attempting to evaluate or improve the writing of others. In addition, chapter 6 ("Dear Writers") includes expanded advice on formatting a manuscript for submission to a publisher, self-editing, and how not to be "difficult."

Introduction

I hear you.

As the editor of *The Chicago Manual of Style Online*'s monthly "Chicago Style Q&A," I've been handling readers' questions about writing style since the University of Chicago Press launched the Q&A in 1997. That amounts to tens of thousands of queries from students, professors, copy editors, business-people, and others who struggle as they write and edit. As of this writing, *The Chicago Manual of Style Online* receives more than a million "page views" per month.[1] Fortunately for us, most visitors do not submit questions to the Q&A.

The Chicago Manual of Style, for the uninitiated, is one of the English-speaking world's most revered style manuals. Although Chicago style may not have the most users, it surely has the most devoted. From its beginnings in the 1890s as a simple in-house sheet of proofreading tips for manuscript editors at the University of Chicago Press to its current online, print, and "mobile optimized" editions, it has grown into a bible for writers and editors in almost every kind of writing outside journalism (where Associated Press style and *New York Times* style dominate).

1. "Analytics *CMOS* Top 50 Pages, Nov. 9, 2014–Feb. 9, 2015," courtesy of Google Analytics.

Written by the Manuscript Editing Department at the University of Chicago Press, *The Chicago Manual of Style* (*CMOS*) has advice on everything from punctuation and capitalization to mathematics and diacritics. Its chapters on the styling of note and bibliography citations have been adopted by universities around the world. Users of *CMOS* include the most impossibly learned writers and editors as well as the most clueless, and for nearly twenty years the monthly Q&A has played host to them all.

Reading the questions that come through the site is a daily adventure away from editing tasks. We answer as many as we can, and I choose the best ones for the monthly posting. The range of topics can be startling. Here's a note we received from the Jet Propulsion Laboratory at NASA:

> **Q** / Dear *Chicago Manual of Style* Q&A Person: What is the rule for sequencing adjectives in a series? For example, we know that numbers come before size indicators (e.g., six small apples). We also know that colors come after size indicators (e.g., six small yellow apples). The specific problem is whether to say "narrow anticyclonically dominated northwestern coast" or "anticyclonically dominated narrow northwestern coast." (Please don't say the correct answer is "anticyclonically dominated northwestern narrow coast"!)

And their kicker ending: "What is the rule that supports your answer?"[2]

---

2. After consulting a linguist, we replied: "Our consultant was somewhat hesitant to comment without a fuller context to work with, suspecting that this may be a 'sentence-level issue and not an adjective-phrase-level issue.' He pointed out that sequencing can vary for reasons of emphasis and that without having the context, he couldn't discern the intended emphasis. If 'narrow' is the emphasis, then it should come first (followed by a comma). If 'anticyclonically dominated' is the emphasis, then it should come first (followed by a comma)."

In contrast, another rather dreamy-sounding note read simply, "Dear *CMOS*, What is Chicago style? Could you give an example?" And one of my favorites: "Would rats die if they drink soda?"

Questions come from all over the world, some from readers who struggle with English. Their grammar questions go deep and are sometimes beyond our ability to respond. ("Please tell differences of *at* and *to*.")

One day this came in:

> **Q** | Hello. I wonder how I can cite the Korean Constitutional Court case. The *CMOS*, as far as I've searched, does not provide a clear tip on it although it spent many pages on the citation rule of U.S., Canadian, and European Court cases. As an illustration, how can I cite "헌법재판소, '대한민국과 일본국간의 재산 및 청구권에 대한 문제 해결과 경제협력에 관한 협정 제3조 부작위 위헌확인' 2006헌마788"?

Recently I learned that a Chinese translation of the 16th edition of the *Manual* has been published. (I wonder what kinds of questions we'll receive once its readers discover the Q&A . . .)

Most of the messages I read, however, are basic questions about style. Often I know the answer, but sometimes I have to look it up—or I e-mail my colleagues for a quick consensus, or I run around and ask the first two or three editors I can find. Although people outside the Press call us "style goddesses" and assume we are experts on everything in the *Manual*, most of the time I feel more like the pathetic little person behind the curtain in *The Wizard of Oz*. It's only because I'm surrounded and protected by knowledgeable and generous coworkers that I can assemble the authoritative front that appears in the Q&A. When I get an esoteric question involving technical writing or linguistics, I can phone or e-mail one of the professors on campus for help. Other times I can do an Internet search and point the reader to a more relevant site.

For the most frequently asked questions, I keep template replies that I can personalize. I can't count the number of times we've been asked whether to type one space or two at the end of a sentence (it's one) or how to cite a tweet (this doesn't worry me as much as it used to). The monthly postings to the Q&A that I cull from all these exchanges are always read by our managing editor and at least two other colleagues, who check my grammar and punctuation and tactfully set me straight when something is wrong.

These days, two categories of questions seem to make up the bulk of the mail. The first type comes from those urgently seeking advice on a writing or an editing issue:

Q | How do I cite a phone conversation with an anonymous caller?

Q | How do you make a proper name and its acronym possessive? The district attorney (DA)'s argument?

Q | *CMOS* lowercases prepositions in book titles, but what if it's a really long one, like "concerning"?

The second type of question comes from readers who want us to settle an argument. In these questions I hear a persistent cry of frustration:

Q | I know I'm right about something. Could *CMOS* please confirm it?

Q | I know I'm right about something. Could you please set my husband/teacher/student/author/colleague/boss/editor straight?

Q | I know I'm right about something. Could you please save the world from its slide into illiteracy?

Questions like these inspired me to write this book, for all of you: for students, professors, copy editors, businesspeople, and writers who are sometimes dogged by indecision or confusion over rules of style and grammar; for those who know the rules but agonize over when or whether to apply them; for those who copyedit for a living and those who don't and those who would like to.[3] In the following pages, I hope to soothe and encourage and lend power. I am not going to do this, however, by setting your teacher/student/author/colleague/boss/editor straight. And I'm not going to help with your homework. You won't learn the fundamentals of copyediting from me. Rather, consider this a "relationship" book, because I'm going to talk about the main relationships in your work life—with the writer, with your colleagues, and with yourself—in ways that you might not have considered before. Ways that might be called subversive.

Right away I should explain what I do *not* mean by a "subversive copy editor," in case anyone has in mind a character

---

3. I will follow *Merriam-Webster's Collegiate Dictionary* (11th ed.) in my spelling of *copy editor* and *copyedit*, *pace* Chicago. And at the risk of annoying some readers, I will use the terms *copy editor* and *manuscript editor* interchangeably. Although their definitions vary, in my mind they are overlapping terms. Copyediting is done by many workers who are not primarily editors—it involves the more or less mechanical reading of copy for spelling, grammar, logic, style, consistency, and appropriate expression. Depending on the worker's level of responsibility, it can be restricted to those functions or allow for greater engagement with the work. Manuscript editing is the work of professional editors. It includes copyediting but may also entail deeper engagement with the content: rethinking, rewriting. It may also encompass administrative responsibilities such as handling copy through stages of production before and after editing, creating and monitoring schedules, or arranging for proofreading and indexing.

like the one my former colleague Joe Weintraub once described in a prize-winning short story. In the story, a snooty language expert named Ezra Peckinpah has been tormented for months by a copy editor who purposely inserts errors into his column at the final stage before printing. In this scene, Ezra has just received the latest issue:

> He held the issue up to the light as if he were inspecting the texture of the paper itself for flaws, and when he found himself beginning the final paragraph with the ungrammatical apostrophe "Just between you, dear reader, and I . . ." his arms twitched outward, his elbow striking his reading lamp so that it tottered on its base and almost toppled to the floor.
>
> "Galleys!" he screamed into the telephone. "I demand to see galleys!"[4]

No—at the risk of disappointing my more twisted readers, let me clarify that my subversive copy editor is an entirely different creature.

Subversive, first, because this editor overthrows the popular view that the writer is a natural adversary competing for power over the prose. In part 1 of this book, I will lay out an alternate view and suggest what I believe to be the most productive order of an editor's loyalties, an order that puts the writer closer to the top of the list and (don't tell my boss) the publishing house closer to the bottom, as they work together in the service of the reader.

Subversive, second, because to live a good life as a copy editor, a person must occasionally think outside the rules. To copyedit is to confront and solve an endless series of problems,

---

4. Joe Weintraub, "The Well of English, Defiled," *Ascent* 10, no. 1 (Fall 1984): 43–57.

great and small. In part 2 of the book, in examining the copy editor's life of conflict, I will zero in on some of the ways we create problems for ourselves even when our writers are expert, thorough, and compliant. You will see how a need to always cleave to the rules can be counterproductive.[5] I will seek to banish the pet compulsions, inflexibilities, and superstitions that get in our way. More than once in these pages, you will read the heretical idea "It's not a matter of being correct or incorrect. It's only a style."

Years ago, in explaining these ideas to my son John, I said I wanted to find ways for everyone to get what they[6] want, sometimes by breaking the rules, and John asked, "Like shoplifting?" Well, no. The idea isn't to allow bad grammar and sloppy attribution of sources. The idea of a good author-editor relationship involves working with writers in ways that will tell you what they really want so you can help them achieve it. A great deal of the time, you'll find that what the writer wants, you want, too. And if you're skilled, your writers will discover that they want most of the same things you do. The second idea, of having good relationships with our colleagues and with ourselves, involves forming work habits and attitudes that allow us to complete our tasks having done the best we can do with the material we were given, without sacrificing more than a little bit of our standards, our sanity, or our sleep.

And who knows? If we're lucky, in the course of figuring out some strategies for getting along with our authors, our bosses,

---

5. If you are rushing off to tweet about that split infinitive—or whatever else you think is in error in this book—may I suggest that you be prepared to cite an authoritative source or two? (I already have mine.) If you find a typo, I'd appreciate knowing of it. But please read chapter 12 before you take to public shaming. One of my goals here is to build a supportive community.
6. See note 5.

our colleagues, and ourselves, we might also happen to learn something more about getting along in life.

· · ·

I am a working editor at the University of Chicago Press, which publishes scholarly books in a wide variety of disciplines. My work has given me contact with people in acquisitions, design, production, and marketing as we go through the mechanics of making books. Since our fifteen full-time in-house manuscript editors aren't enough to handle all the books, we use freelance copy editors as well. Almost all the editing is done electronically using the "track changes" feature in Microsoft Word. In this book I will try to keep in mind that not all of you are working on books or in Word; you aren't all working in-house; you don't all have the flexibility to balk at rules. I devote one chapter to the special concerns of freelancers, and another to those of writers.

In the Manuscript Editing Department at Chicago, although most of the editors have higher degrees, they don't tend to specialize in particular subjects. Manuscripts are usually assigned on the basis of schedule and availability. Over the years, I've landed a three-volume work on the vertebrate skull, a book of Jewish jokes, and a seven-hundred-page bibliography of historical geography. Books that are heavy in math and the physical sciences are usually sent to specialist freelancers. (I once supervised a freelancer who read *Quantum Field Theory in Curved Spacetime and Black Hole Thermodynamics*, a book I kept on my shelf for years to impress visitors.)

Although the bulk of my experience has been in the editing of scholarly books, I have also worked in trade publishing and journalism, and indeed long ago as a secretary, as a clerk/ typist, in data entry, and (just for the record) as a letter carrier.

In all those jobs, I was responsible for writing or editing—or carrying—copy. All this is only to say that I've edited a lot of words and learned a few things along the way that I'd like to share, because you are asking.

In the e-mails seeking help from *The Chicago Manual of Style*, we hear from the frustrated, the panicked, the disaffected. But I like to believe that when we're *not* hearing from them, it's because they're doing just fine, enjoying the pleasures of working at their craft. Knowing how to tinker with a broken piece of prose until it hums is a source of contentment known by all who have mastered a worthy craft. The midwife works with a laboring woman to produce a healthy child. A seamstress or tailor finishes the couturier's garment until it's a perfect, flattering fit. Carpenters and masons execute an architect's vision and take pride in a safe and well-functioning building. What we all have in common is our wish to cooperate—not compete—with the originators of our material, and we share a satisfaction and sense of accomplishment when everything is going well.

Ultimately, I'm hopeful that a reexamination of your role as copy editor—whether that's your title or not—can benefit all parties while liberating you from the oppression of unhelpful habits and attitudes. My point is not how to copyedit, but how to survive while doing it. My hope is to give you some self-assurance and a measure of grace as you go about negotiating one word at a time with the writers you are charged with saving from themselves.

PART ONE

WORKING WITH
THE WRITER,
FOR THE READER

CHAPTER ONE

The Subversive Copy Editor

Q | In a sentence like "the authors thank Natalie and Isabel for her editorial assistance," is it grammatically correct to use the pronoun *her* and not *their*?

WHO ARE YOU?

From reading the letters to *The Chicago Manual of Style Online*'s "Chicago Style Q&A," I'm guessing that many readers of this book are not professional copy editors. But that doesn't mean you don't copyedit. In the routines of almost any office job, a worker is likely to be responsible for a chunk of writing, and in any chunk of writing there is likely to be a problem. Solving problems with writing is what copyediting is. It includes at the very least a review of spelling, grammar, and style, and it often involves checking for accuracy, logic, structure, and elegance of expression. Years ago the periodical *Copy Editor* changed its name to *Copyediting*, for the reason that "the number of those who bear the title 'copy editor' decreases year on year." *Copy Editor*'s editor at the time, Wendalyn Nichols, explained that "more corporations are developing custom publications, and editorial freelancers are branching out beyond the niches they could once remain in quite comfortably. Increasingly, people who edit copy must wear more than one hat."[1] Perhaps as a result, much of the Q&A mail is from workers who aren't trained to copyedit and are looking for guidance.

Anyone who works with the words of others can benefit from advice to professional copy editors. Although I will tend to use the vocabulary I know best, that of a copy editor of book manuscripts, the same tenets can apply in the multitude of contexts where you handle work written by others: newspapers and magazines, corporate and nonprofit materials, online content, newsletters, advertisements, comic books, love letters . . . well, maybe not love letters. Regardless of your title, I invite you to read on.

WHO'S THE BOSS?

When you're faced with a new chunk of writing to tame, you might settle down with your favorite dictionary, your computer open to Google or Bing, *The Chicago Manual of Style* or another style guide, and any other references you use to guide your editing. You might sit in an office with five sharpened pencils on your desk. Or in a basement room, with pizza oozing grease onto the hard copy. You're armed with your own training and inclinations. Maybe your Delete-key finger is itching to stab at extraneous *thats*; maybe you laser in on punctuation. Or maybe you're the big-picture type, ready to put paragraph 1 at the end and write the opener from scratch.

1. Wendalyn Nichols, "Ask *Copy Editor*," in *Copy Editor*, August-September 2007, 4.

Regardless of your modus operandi, when you start in on the process of reading the words and making editorial decisions, you are going to work for *someone*. You'll be vying for that person's approval and striving to meet his or her standards. And that person is . . . the one who hired you? Nope. The writer? Not entirely. Yourself? Not even close.

Your ultimate boss is the *reader*. You, your boss, and your boss's boss all work for the same person, and you all have the same goal of making that person's reading experience the best it can be. I know you saw that coming. Common sense tells us that working on behalf of the reader is not really such a terribly subversive move. After all, that is the mission of the writer and the publisher, even if only for the obvious reason that pleasing readers sells the newspaper, the book, the blog, the widgets. Reassuring and impressing readers keeps them coming back. It persuades them to believe, to invest, to buy.

Since documents have various purposes, it makes sense for editors to tailor them to suit different groups of readers. Whoever hires an editor almost certainly will have a set of rules or guidelines for the editor to follow in doing just that. And when you are obliged to work within guidelines while editing, it's likely that at some point you're going to have to butt heads with someone—whether it's the employer who sets the style or a writer who flouts it. Indeed, editing for the reader routinely involves questioning established rules of style. How could it not? The style used for an article about a photo that "broke the Internet" is not necessarily appropriate for one written about immigration reform. Although the fundamental elements of well-crafted prose are basically the same for all writing, the details are not. A word like "pre-dewatering" can be workaday jargon in a memo about waste treatment—or a witticism in a poem for the *New Yorker*. Numbers like seven thousand three hundred and sixty-two may look fine spelled out once in a novel but would get out of hand in a department budget. Repetition can lend emphasis or organization, or it can just be annoying. Humor doesn't always fit.

Don't be alarmed: I'm not going to suggest that you sass back to your boss, toss out your stylebook, or forget what you know about semicolons and dangling modifiers. On the contrary, I'm going to insist that you know inside and out the rules you're charged with applying and the reasons behind them. Jettisoning a style rule or tenet of good writing doesn't have to mean sacrificing excellence. Rather, it can ensure it. Examples are legion. Here's one: some style guides dictate that upon first mention a person be identified by a full name. In news articles or trade books with an international readership, say, or in school texts destined for readers of mixed abilities and attention spans, the goals are to clarify and educate. Adding *Margaret* to *Thatcher* or *William* to *Shakespeare* isn't likely to patronize and will allow a broader base of readers to follow the text without confusion. In specialized or technical documents, however, directed to a narrow group of experts, a writer might prefer the shorthand of the familiar name alone. In a literary journal article about Renaissance poetry that refers to Dante in passing, adding *Alighieri* might reflect poorly on the writer who states the obvious.

Although it's normal to tinker with a document in order to shape it for the intended reader, you shouldn't automatically expect to make a major overhaul. Fortunately for you, most writers are likely to be better acquainted than you are with the target audience of their work, and you would do well to think before you mess with their choices.

And that brings us to the next issue.

WHOSE COPY IS IT, ANYWAY?

It's good to assume at the outset that a writer has written with her imagined reader in mind. If your writer is an expert, whatever her specialty—computer technology, poetry, fashion—she'll have been steeping in the jargon of that discipline for a while, and she's bound to use it, knowing that it's the best way to communicate with readers who speak the same dialect. Even if she's only recently researched the subject for a commissioned piece, she probably knows more than you do about it. In that way, the writer has already put her reader first, and now she can reasonably expect the editing process to push her prose a little further in the same direction. In her fantasies, your editing will produce a perfect, fascinating work of art. (In her nightmares, you will reduce her work to rubble, but never mind that.) Considering the responsibility this entails, then, let the writer become your second master.

One of the most counterproductive assumptions for young editors to make is that they are going to be working against recalcitrant writers who are ignorant of the rules. Copy editors are sometimes taught to say no, employing the vocabulary of rule enforcement—"It's unconventional," "It's not our style," "It's too expensive," "It will cause a delay." And sometimes we do have to say these things. But to see the writer-editor relationship as inherently adversarial is to doom yourself to a career of angst and stress. The writer's job is far more difficult than the copy editor's: the writer has to actually write the thing. It is your privilege to polish copy without the tedium and agony of producing it in the first place. Your first goal isn't to slash and burn your way through a document in an effort to make it conform to a list of style rules. Your first goal is merely to do no harm.

And oh, baby—the ways in which we do harm.

For every writer with a tin ear who is helped by a competent editor, there is an inexperienced editor who will take a fresh and well-voiced text and edit the life out of it. He'll delete every comma that isn't justified in his high school grammar, and he'll put them in where the writer is trying to pick up speed. He will create tortuous constructions to avoid the passive, and he would lay down his life for a *whom*. For such editors, consistency trumps stylings that give a reader ease and confidence in the writer's authority. These types are obsessed with imposing rules—sometimes rules that are closer to superstitions—that serve only to hamstring the writer and impoverish his prose. It's no wonder they see the writer as a roadblock on the way to the straitened texts they work to achieve.

And then there is a related problem: editors obsessed with the larger issues, wanting a different story, a different argument, a different voice, preferably something closer to their own. Rather than take up the writer's mantle, they cut the cloth to fit themselves.

You might think that overachieving copy editors suffer from knowing too much, but the opposite is true. Knowing too little, they hang on white-knuckled to their small bag of tricks, unaware of the many alternatives.

So the first step in doing no harm is to expand your bag of tricks. A thorough knowledge of the rules and conventions of prose styling will arm you with confidence in choosing the right ones and rejecting the wrong ones. There's a difference between the considered breaking of a rule and a failure to observe it out of ignorance. With the former, you will have a reason and a plan; with the latter, you might just have a mess. You could find yourself blanching at a headline like "Press Recalls Typo-Filled Book and Says It Will Reprint."[2]

If you aren't trained and confident in at least the basics of copyediting, you can't hope to give the readers what they deserve—or gain the respect of your writer.[3] Knowing your stuff, you're ready to serve the reader by working intelligently and sensitively with the writer. If you're charged with following a style guide that you haven't yet mastered, then restraint—doing no harm—is your best tactic.

When you receive a document ready for copyediting, you, more than anyone else, are in a position to champion the writer and protect her project. Nobody else cares as much as you do about that particular work at that particular time. It's likely that no other overseer will read it again before distribution or publication. The editor who acquired it has been there and done that—he's on to courting the next deal. The manager or assigning editor thumbed through it and signed it off to you. The marketer is thinking about it as part of a greater plan; the print buyer isn't engaged with its content much at all. Who, if not you, will be the writer's advocate? If there's a problem—if the fiscal-year projections can't be revised in time, if a book index is too long—everyone benefits if you are

2. *Chronicle of Higher Education News Blog*, article posted May 2, 2008, accessed March 17, 2015, http://chronicle.com/article/Princeton-U-Press-Recalls/40917.
3. There are many ways to acquire knowledge of copyediting through reading books and articles, but as in most undertakings, experience is the best teacher. Chapter 14 includes tips on how to get your foot in the door to a copyediting career. One tip for now: Looking through a style manual will tell you almost instantly whether you really want to be a copy editor, so pay attention to your gut reaction. If you would rather stab yourself with sharp pencils than read it, copyediting may not be for you.

thinking of the project as your own and pushing to get the best of everything for it.

WHY WE MEDDLE

People new to the publishing process might be surprised to learn that there is even such a thing as the copyediting stage. Don't writers proofread and polish and revise before the text is even submitted? Don't acquiring editors critique and send manuscripts to outside readers, and don't the authors refine and update on the basis of the feedback? Isn't the darned thing practically perfect by then?

Well, no.

In academic publishing, a journal article or book manuscript probably goes through more versions, more outside review, and more refining than any other kind of copy by the time it gets to the copy editor. But even so, when the writer and her peers read the manuscript, they tend to focus on the larger picture: the argument, the logic, the organization, and the clarity or accuracy of expression. If peer reviewers spot misspellings or grammar goofs or inconsistencies, they might point them out, but that isn't their mission. A copy editor not only keeps an eye on all that, but he is also taking careful notes and cross-checking hundreds of details. He will keep a style sheet of names and places and decisions to depart from house style. He is going to notice that footnote 43 cites page 12 of a particular article in the *American Journal of Sociology*, whereas the bibliography entry for that article indicates that the article begins on page 22. He recorded on his style sheet that Edward Mulholland appeared on page 51, and he will be suspicious when *Edwin* Mulholland pops up on page 372. He's the one who will find three different spellings of Tchaikowsky/Tchaikovsky/Tchaikovski and that chapter 3 is titled "The Untruth of the Gaze" in the table of contents but "The Untrue Gaze" at the chapter's opening.

In other kinds of publishing, copy will come to you having undergone much less scrutiny, sometimes directly from the writer. A news story may have been madly typed that morning by a stringer on the train to work. Your boss could hand you a letter to potential donors drafted with a Sharpie on the wrapper from her lunch burrito. You may have to start with larger tasks of rewriting before moving on to the finer points of spelling, punctuation, and internal consistency.

Now, I know there are readers among you—maybe those who are only just beginning to contemplate work as a copy editor—who are wondering, "How much does any of this really matter?"

The publishers who hire copy editors obviously believe that it matters a lot. It matters because inaccuracies and inconsistencies undermine a writer's authority, distract and confuse the reader, and reflect poorly on the company. If a page number in the table of contents is wrong, the data in table 4 is just as likely to be wrong. If Mia Wasikowska's name is misspelled, who's going to believe she actually gave the interview? Discriminating readers look for reasons to trust a writer and reasons not to. Sloppy expression and carelessness in the details are two reasons not to. The copy editor's job, then, is to ferret out such infelicities. We do this in order to help the writer forge a connection with the reader based on trust—trust that the writer is intelligent and responsible, and that her work is a reliable source. We do it to help craft an article that pleases, a report that allows the reader to coast along through its ideas without slowing for red lights at every corner. And we do it—

don't we?—because we derive satisfaction and pride from knowing how.

As you read, you will listen for the writer's voice and become her imagined reader, mentally connecting the style of her prose to the message of her pages. You will learn to want what the writer wants, and you will edit to keep her from wandering off the path. When you perceive that what she wants in the moment gets in the way of her greater goals, that's when you step in.

I realize that some copy editors are never given an opportunity to communicate with the writers of the materials they edit. Although this arrangement does have its advantages, it will obviously prevent you from following some of the advice in the first four chapters of this book. I hope you will find the book—and even those chapters—helpful in any case. You, too, have a relationship with your writers, and it can be combative or collaborative, as you wish. You, too, can wish to do no harm; you, too, can listen for the writer's voice and work to protect and promote it.

With this in mind, let's lay the groundwork for an excellent author-editor relationship.

A | If the authors intend to thank both Natalie and Isabel for assistance, then *their* is the right choice. However, if the sentence means "The authors thank Natalie [for something other than assistance, but we aren't saying what] and [we also thank] Isabel for her assistance," then even if it is technically grammatical (debatable), it is nonetheless confusing. (Correct grammar does not mean everything's OK. "Striped sentences wish green habits" is grammatical.) In short, your sentence is a disaster and must be rewritten for clarity.

CHAPTER TWO

The Good Launch

Q | The menu in our cafeteria shows that enchiladas are available "Tues.–Fri." However, when I ordered one on a Wednesday, I was informed that enchiladas are available on Tuesday *and* Friday, not Tuesday *through* Friday. When I informed the cafeteria manager that this was incorrect, she seemed shocked and refused to change the sign. Please help determine who is correct!

THREE VIRTUES OF THE ENLIGHTENED EDITOR

When you are given some copy to edit, the writing comes with a writer attached. Sometimes you're allowed to ignore this fact: the copy will be published without a byline; the writer has little invested in the copy; your contact with the writer will be nil. (Think movie listings in the community newspaper, or lunch menus for the company bulletin boards.) Sometimes, in contrast, you have edited the same writer for years, and you have become, for better or for worse, her helpmate, advisor, coconspirator. (Think the CEO whose letters you type, or the staff writers or columnists for your newspaper or magazine.) If your editor-writer relationships are either of these types—dead-end or committed—you may skip ahead. This chapter is all about when you are thrown together with a new writer and have to figure out how to get along.

Now that I think about it, contacting a writer for the first time is a little like online dating, except that you should be honest. Especially in book editing, it's unusual for an editor to know the writer beforehand, and in many instances, perhaps most, they never meet in person. Why should a writer trust you with his magnum opus? Right off the bat, you will give him three reasons: (1) because your introductory e-mail or phone call shows that you are careful, (2) because you are going to make the process transparent, and (3) because you show no signs of the editorial inflexibility that terrifies writers. *Carefulness, transparency,* and *flexibility*: put these words on your little rubber bracelet. We shall return to them more than once.

Contact the writer after you've looked over the project carefully but before you start editing. The writer is going to be your best ally as you work, so establish cordial relations right away. Unlike at OkCupid, you will at least know his real name, which makes it easier to find out something about him ahead of time. Go ahead and Google: your approach to him and his work can only benefit by knowing his interests and how he presents himself online. On the phone or in an e-mail, show that you've familiarized yourself with his manuscript (best not to mention the Googling part) by asking a question or two, and let the questions show your knowledge and competence. Be sure to introduce yourself while you're at it. If you are particularly interested in or have special experience in his topic, let him know.

If you're able, express sincere enthusiasm about the project.

Tell the writer your proposed schedule and give him whatever contact information you want him to have. (Think twice about the cell phone number—although I've given mine several times and never regretted it.) If relevant, ask if he prefers to be contacted by e-mail or phone and whether he minds your asking questions occasionally while you're reading, rather than all at once at the end. Once you've written this sort of e-mail a few times in your own words, you'll have a template for introductions that you can tailor to each new author.

> Dear Ms. Writer:
> [Introductory template blah-blah.]
> Finally, before I begin editing, I have a question for you. I notice you consistently cap Impressionism, but otherwise I don't see a clear system in your casing of art styles and movements: baroque, classic, romantic, cubist, modern (plus their -ists and -isms). Our style is to lowercase, but before I meddle, please let me know whether I should, and if so, your preferences.

One good question like this will show the writer that you will pay attention to detail as you whip her stuff into shape. (This is carefulness.) It reassures her that you'll make no sudden moves without her knowledge. (Transparency.) And it demonstrates your willingness to listen and negotiate. (Flexibility.) But several additional benefits may result from introducing yourself in this manner. From a writer's response, you might gain important information about her attitudes and preferences. You'll see right away whether she's relaxed or worried about someone whose red pen is poised over her text. She'll make demands—or ask questions of her own. You'll note how prompt she is in getting back to you, and whether she is curt or long-winded or funny. At the very least, you'll save yourself work later searching for every mention of baroque, classic, romantic, cubist, modern (plus their *-ists* and *-isms*) in order to reinstate the meticulous system of capping that she had checked and rechecked before submitting her copy, all of which you decided to lowercase without asking. (In the case of the capped art movements, I was so surprised by a famous writer's willingness to leave everything to me, I wrote back impulsively, "I was actually half hoping you'd be pompous and dictatorial and solve the problem by insisting on one way or another." The writer replied, "I'm sorry to have missed an opportunity to be pompous and dictatorial.")

SIX HABITS TO CULTIVATE—NOW

When you're ready to begin editing, wait a second. The start of a new project is a heady moment. So far, so good—you haven't even had a chance to do harm. The writer has confidence in you. This is the time to remind yourself of six good habits that will prolong the honeymoon, or at least make damage control easier if disaster strikes.

1. *Ask first, and ask nicely.* We've already agreed on some benefits of asking questions before you begin tinkering: they showcase your capability, they can save you work later, and the writer's answers give you clues to her personality and preferences. But in managing your relationship with a writer, questions serve another important purpose: they foster a collaborative environment rather than an adversarial one. For this reason, it's good to frame your questions positively rather than negatively, even when you can hardly believe what you're seeing in the copy. Resist writing little passive-aggressive hints that

the writer is lazy or that her work isn't up to your standards. ("Your capitalization seems to change in every paragraph. I'm sure you know what you're doing—I'm sorry I can't figure out your system. Would you mind explaining?") And I won't even mention the tail-covering benefits of asking first. (We'll get to that later.)

2. *Don't sneak (much)*. If you're editing electronically, you'll probably use a feature called tracking, or redlining, which shows your changes in a way that keeps the original visible at the same time. For instance, if you insert text, it might appear underlined, <u>like this</u>; when you delete text, it might have a line through it, ~~like this~~.[1] Because you can turn the tracking feature on and off at will, you have the option of altering the text "silently," that is, with the feature turned off. Some types of uncontroversial changes are not easy to display visually through tracking (such as eliminating double and triple spaces accidentally typed between words), so it makes sense to make them silently. You want the redlined copy to be as readable as possible. Some kinds of tracked changes, like the removal of hyphens or the deletion of an *s* at the end of a word, can be visually- confusing (see what I mean?). You could just change them—what the heck—and not say anything. But it's better to note such changes the first time ("-*ly* adverbs unhyphenated silently hereafter"). Keep a list of the types of silent changes you make, and send it along with the edited copy. Other good candidates for silent editing include the deletion of hyphens after prefixes, the change of hyphens to en dashes in inclusive

---

1. Be aware that the way tracked changes appear in a document is determined by each user's computer settings at the time of reading. You will frustrate and confuse writers by referring to changes "in red" or "underlined" or "in the comments balloon," without adding "depending on your settings." Offer to talk them through changing their settings if it's important for their view to match yours.

numbers, and the addition of formats or styles. I note in my cover letter that I made such uncontroversial silent changes per *CMOS* and our house dictionary.

3. *Eliminate surprises.* If you steer clear of stealth-editing, you will eliminate one type of unpleasant surprise for your writer, but without adequate warning other shockers can arise, unrelated to the content of your editing. You might send her the editing just as she's leaving for two weeks of incommunicado research for a cover story on gorilla tracking in Central African Republic. Or you might discover that a writer assumed wrongly that she could add illustrations at a later stage. Here is actual e-mail correspondence with a writer who was surprised to learn that he was responsible for indexing his book:

> **AU** | What index? Haven't I sent it already?
>
> **ED** | You sent a list of entries, but you need to add the page numbers—and in the proper format, as I mentioned. You'll have to take a pass through the pages to find the page numbers. This is not generated automatically, unfortunately.
>
> **AU** | This must be a mistake. Why can't it be done automatically? You guys have the electronic files, so why should it be done manually and by me?

Fortunately for you, all these things have happened to me, so they needn't happen to you. When you first make contact with a writer, list all the deadlines you know, and ask about travel or teaching plans that could cause problems. (If you're editing news copy, your deadline issues will be very different, and your writers will probably already understand them.) Confirm who is responsible for proofreading or indexing, and if you learn that the writer intends to hire a freelancer for either chore, warn that freelancers typically book weeks in advance.

Make sure the writer understands how long changes or additions to the copy or illustrations will be possible.

4. *Check in.* As the project progresses, take other opportunities to remind the writer of impending transactions. E-mail is a perfect tool for this. ("Hello—just checking in. Have you had a chance to look at the editing? Is everything clear?" "Hello—just wanted to let you know I expect page proofs in a couple of weeks, and to confirm that you're ready to read them. I'll be giving you until July 17 to get them back to me. I hope this is good timing—please let me know if you foresee any problems.")

Even in the age of digital proofs, you might have to send out hardcopy for proofreading, which means tracking packages and double-checking the writer's receipt of them. Even if you receive notice of delivery from the carrier company, authors sometimes leave a package unopened until they're ready to work on it, so you can't rely on the cover letter you put in the package to communicate the deadline. I once e-mailed to nudge a translator who was a bit late returning page proofs, and she replied, "When are they due? I haven't opened them yet." For this reason, it's good to give the writer the deadlines in an e-mail or phone call at the same time you send the package, and when you receive notice of delivery, ask the writer to confirm. Just because someone at CyberWidgets signed for it, that doesn't mean it's not languishing in a corner of the mailroom.

Checking on a writer is easier if your instructions were clear in the first place and if you prepared him for the next steps. When a writer is reviewing your editing, it's important for him to know how much he can change and whether this is his last chance to make changes. Your cover-letter template should stress this. ("Finally, this is the time to make all your last corrections. At page-proof stage, changes can be expensive and even risky, since they sometimes cause additional errors, and you will not have a chance to proof the revisions." A former boss and mentor of mine used to add something like "Sorry to sound bossy—it just seems a good idea to prevent disappointment later.")

5. *Keep it professional.* There are bound to be times when you and a writer click so well that your working relationship edges toward friendship, and I'm not going to tell you to slam the door on that. But I will point out that being the writer's advocate is not the same as being his buddy. As long as you are handling his work, your first loyalty is going to be to the reader, and there will be times when a little professional distance will make this easier. It's not unheard of for a writer to develop, let's say, personal-boundaries issues with an editor: one writer sent a colleague of mine a photo of himself wearing a fake (she hopes) tattoo of a heart with her name in it. What's more, as another colleague reminded me, "If you're extra nice, they take advantage of you."

In this vein, professionalism begins the first time you write to "Dear Mr. Surname," not to "Dear Bob." Although some of the young people I talk to think this courtesy has gone the way of the dinosaurs, the fact is that in publishing the dinosaurs are often calling the shots, and if you annoy one, it's your problem. If Mr. Surname writes back "Yours, Bob," then fine. (One of my colleagues was charmed by a courtly southern author who, after months of intense collaboration from a distance, wrote, "I am now ready to call you Leah, if you would call me Beauregard.")

We'll talk more about e-mail management later, but in the context of maintaining a professional demeanor, make it an unbreakable rule (even at the risk of blowing your reputation as a subversive) to reply promptly to a writer's query whether you know the answer or not. It takes only a few seconds to reassure her that you're listening. ("Beth, I'm sorry I don't know—I'll find out ASAP.") Apologize freely for lapses or delays, but don't explain them in more than vague terms. Complain to your dog that you got slammed with three deadlines more pressing than Beth's. To Beth, you're simply sorry it took a while to get back to her. The idea is to strike a balance between having the author think she's the center of your world and revealing that she's actually one of many. In short, never whine. At the office, anyway.

Let me expand on that last point: it's rarely a good idea to explain anything more than is absolutely necessary. That's counterintuitive, because our first impulse is to appease, to defend ourselves, to receive permission, to *explain*. But when you mention specifics, you provide ammunition for rebuttal on each point. In a first-level explanation, it's better to be firm but vague. Be professional. In giving you the following personal example, I will humiliate myself. But (1) I want to save you from making similar mistakes, and (2) I want you to know that I don't pretend to be the perfect, together, blissed-out editor. Just the opposite: I mess up *all the time*. It's how I know things. So here's an e-mail I once drafted to the organizer of a webinar who kept increasing her demands on my time until I felt I could no longer participate.

"BEFORE" VERSION: Gertrude, I'm very sorry, but I fear that I'm not a good fit for your webinar. I had a hunch from the beginning that I was too clueless about the corporate setting to meet your expectations, and this confirms it. You assumed I'd have slides and never even thought to mention it, whereas it wouldn't have occurred to me in a million years. I've never made a slide in my life and have no idea how slides could possibly enhance my remarks.

You seem to be expecting a presentation of some kind, and I simply don't have the time or motivation to provide one. I'm so sorry—I agreed as a courtesy to make a few remarks about the *Manual of Style* for your webinar, and I tried to stress that I wouldn't have more than a few minutes of thoughts about the importance of editing to a style. Quite frankly, I have to keep in mind that the U of C Press isn't invested in your product and you aren't paying for my time, and it would simply be wrong for me to spend more than a few minutes preparing for the event. I don't even have that kind of time on top of my responsibilities here.

I'm afraid I have to bow out. Again, my sincere apologies for the misunderstanding. I hope the event goes well.

And here's the note I actually sent, after my boss read the drafted e-mail and frowned. "Don't explain," she said. Oops—right.

"AFTER" VERSION: Gertrude, I'm very sorry, but I'm afraid my schedule and responsibilities are going to force me to withdraw from your webinar. I hope this news comes in time for you to recruit another speaker. I'm sorry for any inconvenience. I wish you all the best.

6. *Say "Yes."* One of the great things—perhaps the only great thing—about being low on the totem pole of publishing power is that there is a lot you don't get to decide, which means that you also don't have to say no. Instead, you can say, "I'll ask." If a writer says that he wants his favorite aunt to rewrite his contract and his seven-year-old to supply the illustrations, write

back that, wow, you aren't sure it can happen, but you'll get right on it. Then do your part to pass along his requests—as earnestly as you can—to the person who will tell him no. When a writer's request is reasonable but outside your control, take your best case to whoever can decide. Remember that you are probably the person most familiar with the work and therefore able to judge whether the writer's request has merit. Choose your battles well. If you consistently approach your colleagues or superiors with good ideas, you'll gain credibility and respect not only with the author but with them as well.

There are many times, of course, when you yourself will have to decide and your inclination may be to say no. I always have that impulse when a writer wants to reinstate something I consider a solecism. Even so, we discuss it until both sides are satisfied. I listen to the writer's justification; I offer evidence or examples from my authorities; and in most cases it quickly becomes clear that one of us has the better case.

EVERYBODY WINS

So far this is a pretty rosy picture. You've got your act together, the writer is jazzed to receive great editing from your capable hands, and all involved will get what they want: The reader will get a terrific read; the writer will win critical praise and royalties; and the publisher will rake in prestige and profits. You, in your quiet, anonymous way, will have the reward of a job well done and pride in contributing to the world's store of good literature.

But maybe you're thinking, "Easy for her to say," and wondering exactly how you're supposed to communicate carefulness, transparency, and flexibility to your author; how you're supposed to maintain all those habits when you're elbow-deep in a project. (Not to mention how you manage when you have the Copy from Hell.) So in the next chapter, let's take a closer look.

A | Although the sign was incorrect, I'm not sure you should annoy the person who provides the enchiladas.

CHAPTER THREE

Working for the Reader, through the Writer

CAREFULNESS, TRANSPARENCY, FLEXIBILITY

Q / When the original author of a book has died and the original book is being revised by others, what is the best way to handle this on the title page? Should the original author be mentioned at all?

In chapter 2, I suggested that carefulness, transparency, and flexibility are the three paths to editing enlightenment. Let's take a closer look at how each of these can benefit both ourselves and our writers.

CAREFULNESS

Being careful while editing is a worthless gesture if you don't know what you're doing. A young editor I once supervised was extravagantly careful in inserting about a thousand commas to separate author and date in parenthetical source citations (e.g., Edwards, 1981). If he had taken that much care in studying *CMOS*, he would have known that Chicago style omits the comma. If he had known even a little bit more, he would have decided to leave it alone regardless of Chicago style.

The point is, when I talk about carefulness, I am also talking about the application of knowledge. If you don't know the issues, trends, and rules of style and grammar, you won't be aware of all the little things that might or might not need attention. You can be the most meticulous person in the world as you start reading, but if you are ignorant of the issues, you will happily read past problems that should set off alarms. So the first step toward carefulness is to study your style manual. If it's a chunky doorstop like *CMOS*, it might be a gradual process, but keep your guide handy and make a habit of referring to it.[1] If a specific guide is not required for your work, pick one that appeals to you. And if you are new to editing, remember your mantra: "First do no harm."

A trove of knowledge, don't forget, exists in your author. She may be clueless about the style you are following, but she probably has two kinds of expertise that you may not: she

---

1. Here's some concrete advice for learning a style manual, in reply to a reader who wrote to ask whether there was a tutorial program for studying *CMOS*:

> A / Try not to be intimidated. Unless you're a technical writer, you can ignore some of the chapters and use them only for occasional reference. The goal is to know what's in the book and how to find it, not to memorize it. Start by skimming the chapter on manuscript preparation and editing, and if it applies to the work you're doing, read it more closely. Then look through the chapters on punctuation and spelling. Again, the important thing is to educate yourself on the issues, not necessarily all the various solutions. Scan through the chapter on names and terms, so you'll know when you need it. (You will surely linger over "Titles of Works.") Read the introduction to the chapter on numbers, and if it holds your interest, keep reading. Look at the book's table of contents and the individual chapter TOCs to see what issues apply to your own work. When you're feeling strong, tackle the chapters on source citation—where the real copy editors hang out. After that, just dip in when you encounter things you need to know. To some, the book's a page-turner; you may find yourself browsing, especially if you have the online edition.

knows her subject, and she probably knows her reader. In most editing projects, there will be issues you should leave to the writer, and doing so doesn't hurt your credibility. It would hurt your credibility to pretend you are fluent in Yorùbá. But don't just shove everything into her lap ("Please remember that no one here will check the Yorùbá"). Do your part. Pay close attention and figure out whether the writer has been careful or not, and prod her if necessary. ("Please check all the Yorùbá. I notice some variation in the diacritics and in the way words are combined in otherwise identical phrases. These may be intentional, but I have no way to tell: *orí kí*, *oríkí*, *òrí kì*, or *oríkì*? There is also variation in upper- and lowercasing of terms. Perhaps you could answer my questions in your glossary first, and once the glossary is the way you want it, check the article against it as you read. I'm enclosing my style sheet for reference.")

Although we must credit the writer's knowledge of her field and her audience, don't assume she's up on every subtlety of grammar and style and will immediately recognize the wisdom of your corrections. If you make changes you think the writer might reject out of ignorance, especially if you appear to be introducing an inconsistency, explain why at the first instance. ("Chicago lowercases 'the board,' but uppercases 'Board of Trade,' hereafter silently.") Sometimes in my cover letter, I prepare a writer up front for my editing of a pervasive problem:

> When I query your choice or spelling of a word, it's often because I can't find support for it in a dictionary. In the case of technical jargon, please write *stet* to keep your original.[2] But

---

2. *Stet* is Latin for "Let it stand."

if you think other readers might also be confused, consider glossing the term.

In this way, I try to demonstrate care and attention: I identify an editing issue and express an informed preference. When appropriate, I let the writer decide.

A brief digression here on the importance of careful querying. Care in editing is demonstrated by the quality of the changes you suggest, but the impression given by excellent line editing can be undone by ill-considered queries to the writer. For this reason, craft your questions with care. Three ways to do that:

1. *Don't bother writers with questions they can't answer.* One of my trainees used to look up every compound phrase and challenge the writer if it didn't match her dictionary: "*double header* (open) as intended?"; "*cut-off* (hyphenated) as intended?"; "*bone shop* (open) as intended?"; "*salt water* (open) as intended?"; "*kow-tow* (hyphenated) as intended?" If I'd been the writer, I would have wondered whether I was being machine-edited. I would rather have seen the editor's decisions, tracked, along with a note in the cover letter that compounds were edited per a specified dictionary.

One editor I supervised asked an author to check the original source of a quotation because the casing of "National Socialist party" didn't match our house style (Party), which was used in the rest of the book. This was unreasonable. (If a quote says "National Socialist *pastry*," then fine—send the writer to the library to check the original.) Another editor challenged an italic phrase within a book title: "Is this a genre or the title of something?" I understood that the editor wanted to make sure the phrase was "correctly" styled with quotation marks or reverse italics, but the author probably had no idea why she was being asked about it. It's a subtle difference, and few readers would know or care what difference the styling conveyed. Was it really worth everyone's time and patience to worry about an arbitrary style to that degree? Such queries can quickly overwhelm a writer, who might rightly feel harassed and question the editor's judgment. If the title was styled consistently throughout, the editor was only making trouble by querying. It's better to save queries for when there's actual trouble to shoot.

2. *Be brief. Don't patronize or overexplain.* Explanations should be used sparingly. It's tedious for a writer to read endless justifications of the editing, especially when they consist of Delphic citations like "Per *CMOS* 14.180" or "See *OED* s.v." That will only show your insecurities. Save the explanations for when you actually have to defend one of your decisions.

3. *Read over the early queries when you're finished.* You will almost always be glad you did. Many editing decisions at the beginning of a document turn out to be the wrong ones in light of what followed; you will know and understand the writer and the content better when you've finished reading. You may want to adjust your tone accordingly.

To review, carefulness means making use of knowledge: your own knowledge of style and grammar, plus the writer's knowledge of the topic and the audience. One last type of knowledge resides in your own experience as a reader, so don't hesitate to reference it in your explanations and queries. You've spent your whole life reading newspapers, magazines, books, and websites, noticing their ambiguities and lapses of logic. You've often wished you could ask a writer to elaborate or rephrase for clarity. This is your chance. Explain briefly why your more subtle changes are not gratuitous: *"because you haven't introduced Stanpole yet"* or *"I stumbled here, taking 'pic-*

ture' as a verb." Use your own experience to suggest changes
that will help the generalist reader, if it's appropriate.

TRANSPARENCY: THE SEE-THROUGH DOCUMENT

Since we've already seen many examples of how one edits
transparently, I can be brief here. We let the writer know ahead
of time what we're going to do, and we ask questions before
we meddle in murky areas. We mark corrections and queries
clearly as we go, using the tracking feature of our word processors as well as written explanations of potentially controversial decisions. And we summarize our decisions in a letter
of editorial notes or a style sheet that we send with the edited
copy. Transparency happens before, during, and after; and at
all three stages it invites the participation of the writer. Indeed, the purpose of transparency is to involve the writer in
a collaboration rather than present the edited copy as a fait
accompli.

Many copy editors, especially freelancers, may not have
the opportunity to talk or e-mail with a writer while editing.
Instead, you work through an intermediary. But that doesn't
mean you get to exclude the writer from your process. Although you may have to make unilateral decisions for the sake
of forging ahead, you can observe the same habits of care,
transparency, and flexibility as you work. Whether it's your
project editor, your boss, or the commissioning agent, there
is usually someone who has requested your services and who
will serve as a surrogate for the writer, either by helping you
make important decisions or by asking the writer on your behalf. If you eventually get the edited copy back from the writer

for the cleanup stage, you will read her responses and copyedit any additions and corrections. If you are careful, transparent, and flexible as you work, the odds are better that the writer will be receptive to your editing, and you will have fewer loose ends to negotiate at that stage.

My best advice related to transparency paradoxically involves something unexpressed: it's about what you will be ready to do if called upon. The two tips that follow just might be the most important advice in this book:

- *In editing*, every time you make a mark on someone else's copy, you must know why, according to an authority, chapter and verse, you are making that change. (You needn't actually cite the reason, which would be obnoxious. Do that only when you anticipate trouble over a popular grammar misconception or a perceived inconsistency.)
- *In querying*, every time you challenge a writer's grammar, usage, or facts, you must first either look it up, remember looking it up, or (if it's one of those evolving issues) remember looking it up in the not-too-distant past.

If you do all that, you still might not always be right, but you'll be ready for intelligent discussion, and your odds of looking like an idiot will be significantly reduced.

FLEXIBILITY: A STYLE IS JUST A STYLE

Of the three virtues I'm touting, flexibility is perhaps the most difficult for a copy editor to embrace. Carefulness almost goes without saying. By nature we are meticulous—you are probably insulted that I would even bother to mention the need for care in editing. And transparency is easier than ever to manage with the use of redlining software. But I know from reading the "Chicago Style Q&A" mail over the years that when it comes to our editing decisions, it can be very, very difficult to be "flexible" when that seems to mean sacrificing something we believe in. When we know a rule and have taken pains to impose it consistently throughout a document only to meet with the writer's resistance, our instinct is to go down fighting. It's a matter of honor. Of professional pride. And maybe even, just a little bit, of power. "My author insists on . . ." is one of the most frequent openers to Q&A readers' style questions. The very wording tells me that you are locked in a battle of wills. And by god, we have our standards.

There are several reasons I'd like you to reconsider this kind of inflexibility, and none of them involves the loss of virtue. For starters, by far the majority of the issues involved in routine copyediting concern style, rather than grammar or documentation. A huge number of you write to *CMOS* for confirmation that a particular style rule is "correct":

Q | My boss wants to cap "Department" when he writes "The department meeting is Thursday," and he won't believe me when I tell him this is wrong.

Q | I want to delete the space after a colon in journal citations, per *CMOS* (e.g., *Social Networks* 14:213–29), but my author disagrees. Can you please back me up on the correct style?

Q | I just got a manuscript back from an author who stetted every hyphen that I had deleted from words with prefixes (postindustrial, pre-war, etc.). I know it's correct to close them up, but his dictionary shows them with hyphens. I'm completely confused. Has this rule changed?

What these questions suggest is that copy editors fail to understand that style rules (which pertain to punctuation, capitalization, hyphenation, preferred spellings, and conventions for citing sources, among other things) are often by nature arbitrary and changeable. If style rules were universal and immutable, there would be no need for different style guides and dictionaries. Although grammar (which governs subject-verb agreement, use of pronouns, sequence of tenses, and so forth) also changes over time, it does so much more slowly, often amid controversy. Many contexts allow for informal grammar or even slang, but grammar rules are generally more strict and less negotiable than those of style.

The inability to identify the difference between negotiable matters of style and less negotiable matters of English grammar is perhaps the most common cause of grief among those who send in questions to the Q&A. Not only are there many different and competing sets of style rules (*The Chicago Manual of Style* is only one of them), but they are different for a reason. For instance, the Associated Press (AP) style used by newspapers is based on selling newspapers to the masses. It promotes vocabulary accessible to readers of varying educational backgrounds. It avoids politically charged language, striving for a neutral and unbiased tone. The publishers of educational materials for children have similarly purposeful style guides; the most rigid ones include word lists for each grade level and limit the number of words in a sentence.

The style guidelines in *CMOS* have accumulated over the years according to their popularity and usefulness in scholarly writing. They change from one edition to the next when they are no longer helpful. In the sixteenth edition, we decided to give up on the 9 January 1930 style and write dates the way most Americans do: January 9, 1930. We put the *n* back in *2nd*.

In the fourteenth edition, ahead of our time in a matter where style intrudes upon grammar, we recommended using *their* as a nonsexist pronoun in singular contexts: Anyone could have forged their signature on that check.[3] We constantly argue over whether to kill off the en dash. And we have stated in every edition since the first in 1906 that "rules and regulations such as these, in the nature of the case, cannot be endowed with the fixity of rock-ribbed law. They are meant for the average case, and must be applied with a certain degree of elasticity."

The point is, your style guide—or any given style "rule" you learned in school—was created so you would do something the same way every time for the sake of consistency, for the reader's sake. It's less distracting that way. You learn style rules so you don't have to stop and ponder every time you come to a number in the text: "Hmm. Here's a number. Shall I spell it out?" You know your chosen style by heart, so you just fly by with confidence. Style rules aren't used because they're "correct." They're used for your convenience in serving the reader.

Although there are certainly some style conventions that are just as ironclad as the most accepted grammar and syntax rules, on the whole style is far more negotiable than you might believe.[4] If a writer has a preference that you can tolerate, consider doing so. If there's a reason why that style is inappropri-

---

3. At the time, we relegated the suggestion to a footnote; in the fifteenth and sixteenth editions, we omitted it altogether—only later to see the singular *they* gain widespread adoption in the popular press and increasing approval by linguists and language writers as the most elegant solution for avoiding "he or she" in sentences like the example in the text.

4. If you are copyediting for a professional journal, newspaper, or magazine, you may have very little flexibility in the styling of citations and certain other editorial tasks. But then, your writer won't be allowed to object to these styles, either.

ate for the document, make your arguments and perhaps the writer will see reason.

Grammar is less negotiable than style. Flouting the rules of grammar creates an impression that the writer is incompetent or uneducated. Most writers are grateful when we correct their grammar. Style is different. Flexibility in imposing style and in many other matters, then, is one of the key tools to managing good relationships with your writers. By indicating that your editing will be open to discussion, you give a writer reassurance that will inform your relationship from the start. I would never compare working with writers to parenting toddlers, but every parent knows that laying down the law is not often the smartest strategy, whether you are negotiating with a toddler or a teen. In editing, as in life, I have found "We can discuss this" to be a reliably effective suggestion. Sometimes the other party thinks, "Oh, well, since I have a choice, I'll let it go," and sometimes, "Omigod—she wants to 'discuss' this. I'd rather just let it go."

If the idea of flexibility in editing alarms you—if you have doubts about its feasibility, results, or morality—I suggest you go straight to chapter 5 for further persuasion.

. . .

By now we have spent three chapters preparing for our work with a writer or the writer's surrogate. We've arranged our priorities and established cordial communications; we've internalized some good habits; we have "Carefulness, Transparency, and Flexibility" tastefully tattooed somewhere upon our persons, or at least upon our psyches; we're doing whatever we can to master and retain knowledge of our house style. We're ready for anything.

But are we? In the next chapter, let's start facing our worst fears.

A | Horrors! When writers die, others don't get to grab their stuff and claim it belongs to them. The original writer is the *only* one whose name is required on the title page; the revisers' names are optional. If they want to be on a title page, tell them to write their own stuff.

CHAPTER FOUR

When Things Get Tough

THE DIFFICULT AUTHOR

Q / Oh, English-language gurus, is it ever proper to put a question mark and an exclamation mark at the end of a sentence in formal writing? This author is giving me a fit with some of her overkill emphases, and now there is this sentence that has both marks at the end.

Although bad things can happen to good editors with no warning, there are other times we feel in our bones that trouble's ahead. Sometimes we sniff danger in the writing; sometimes we sense it in the writer. In any case, it will be useful to identify resources for coping under siege conditions and have them at the ready.

Over my entire career in editing, I don't think I've encountered half a dozen difficult authors. By "difficult," I mean a writer who simply does not want changes made to his work and is not even prepared to discuss them. We know the stereotypes: The hotshot journalist jealous of every comma. The poet who claims that his misspellings and eccentric punctuation are inspired. Assistant professors writing a first book for tenure are notorious for their inflexibility, and understandably so: their futures are at stake. They take editing personally; red marks on their manuscripts are like little stab wounds. And then there are vain authors who quarrel when we lowercase their job titles, who want their photos plastered all over the piece or their names in larger type. And don't get me started on writers who don't know what they're talking about, writers who are your boss, writers who are former high school English teachers.

One freelance editor told me of a writer who rejected all her editing because he wanted to be "deliberately obscure." Another edited a historian who insisted that the dashes in his subject's handwritten notebooks were of seven different lengths that had to be differentiated in typesetting. I once edited a philosopher who fussed that his entire argument would become nonsensical if the book design didn't include little ornaments (>>><<<) in the line spaces. Probably the most startling story I've heard was about a freelance copy editor for a women's magazine who discovered that her writer—a famous "domestic diva"—had plagiarized a recipe. The poor freelancer mysteriously died the very same night she invited the writer to a dinner party at her house . . .

But I don't mean to worry you. Statistically speaking, I believe that the number of copy editors murdered by their authors is fairly low. In my experience, in fact, the more published the writer, the more tolerant and even grateful he is for the copy editor's help. He already knows how much embarrassment we can save him, and he's often busy with other projects and glad to pass the baton at the end stages of this one. The exception, of course, is a published writer who's been burned before by bad editing. (What—like it doesn't happen?)

Our task, regardless, is not to analyze the writer's insecurities but to provide the best product possible for the reader. When you sense from your opening communications that a writer may be resistant to editing, crank up the precautions we've already discussed in order to smooth the way.

CARE TO THE NTH

As always, our watchwords are carefulness, transparency, and flexibility. Faced with a nervous author, you will save yourself much grief if right from the start you limit your expectations and work accordingly. Be conservative in your editing. Summon all the generosity you can, keeping in mind that this writer may have a take on his readers that you don't necessarily understand. Long ago in my first editing job at a popular national magazine, one of my tasks was to copyedit the movie review column of Judith Crist. A veteran writer with a huge and zealous following, Crist took pride in producing columns that needed no editing. Normally, she responded to the copyediting by phone through her assistant. She would tell the assistant what to say, and the assistant would say it into the phone; I would reply, and the assistant would relay the reply to Mrs. Crist (her preferred appellation). The process was clumsy, but better than the alternative: in my ignorance of her quirky habits and favorite phrasings, I often made changes that would cause her to rip the phone away from the assistant to yell at me. I soon learned to leave her writing alone and stick to fact-checking, and even then I would query rather than risk her wrath. The rare times I found a typo or factual error, she ceded the point graciously, and gradually I was permitted to make an occasional tweak in syntax or word choice. After a year or so we ended up getting along well, and when I eventually left that job, she sent me a charming letter of thanks.

As you take extra care to do no harm, keep track of everything you do in case you have to undo it later. If you run macros or other cleanup chores or make global corrections or style changes without tracking turned on (as is sometimes the best course), make a note of everything you did. If early on you see that the copy needs heavy editing or cutting and you fear the response, send a sample for the writer's approval. Consider sending two versions: one with the tracked editing visible and a second, clean copy.[1] When I do this, I stress my reassurances: the sample is for the purpose of deciding how to proceed; everything is negotiable. ("I suggest you read the clean version first to see whether the text reads well in spite of the cuts. Then please look at the deleted material to see whether something critical must be restored.") If your editing and cutting have been judicious, the writer will likely recognize it and direct you to carry on. If he's appalled, you'll have to ask for detailed feedback and work from there. Either way, the idea is to disarm the writer with your willingness to cooperate.

Remember especially my advice from chapter 3: always know why, according to an authority, you are making a change; and always, before querying something unfamiliar, look it up. Some writers will tolerate your twiddling with their prose in ways you think "sound better." The difficult writer will not.

If you're sending heavily edited copy without a preview, take the precaution of explaining some of the editing issues and emphasize your willingness to discuss them. Name the style guide and dictionary you used as arbiters in questions of consistency. Try to prevent the writer from simply saying no without addressing the issues. ("I rarely meddled unless there was a problem with grammar or syntax or consistency of style, so if you don't like my solution to a particular problem, it will be helpful if you can suggest an alternative.")

---

1. Never assume someone knows how to hide the tracking in a document.

Finally, be careful not to promise a writer anything you don't have the authority to promise. A managing editor I know told me horror stories of book editors who, without checking first, allowed pushy authors to add a chapter, submit additional illustrations, and extend the deadline. These are serious gaffes in publishing—substantive additions must be vetted at a higher level. Art can blow a budget and affect everything from printing costs to publication date. Delays can sometimes be tolerated, but other times they ruin everything from book signings to award nominations to time-sensitive marketing plans. These are often contractual issues, not up to the copy editor's discretion. Remember: when requests from an intimidating author will affect a project's cost or schedule, you don't always have to say no; you just have to be careful about saying yes.

EXAMINING YOUR MOTIVES

Perhaps I should pause here to point out that writers aren't the only ones with ego issues. Copy editors tend to be smart and educated, and you have mastered a body of arcane style and grammar knowledge that you apply daily in your work. You take pains to make good decisions, and when a writer rejects your decisions, your first response might be to take it personally, as an insult. If a writer pens rude replies on the copy, it's natural to feel annoyed or even angry. Oh, yes—we've all seen them: "I wrote it that way because I want it that way," "No!!! Stet!!!," or (true story) even "Bullshit." One Chicago manuscript editor had an author who wrote in the margin, "No, don't make this change." A few pages later he wrote, "I told you not to make this change." By the end of the book he was writing, "HOW MANY TIMES DO I HAVE TO TELL YOU, DON'T MAKE THIS CHANGE!" (We hoped he was just trying to be funny.)[2]

It's natural to want to assert your authority and win the point. But it simply doesn't do any good to let those feelings have their way. It's better to stay objective, even if you have to resort to mind tricks to calm yourself: *I did my job. It's his byline, not mine. My colleagues will sympathize when I rail about this. This will make a great dinner-party story. Someday I'll write a book.*

I'm not suggesting that you let yourself be battered into submission when a writer is clearly wrong about something. My point is rather that when you decide to argue, it should be on the merits of the point, not because you feel you have something to prove. Likewise, don't let a writer's mistreatment of you color your opinion of his every decision. Even jerks can be right sometimes.

The last thing you want to do is ruin the chances for a civil collaboration. You aren't infallible yourself—remind yourself that a haughty reply will do nothing to ease tension or reassure the writer.

DEALING WITH BULLIES

When a writer's response to your editing borders on the belligerent, you may have a bully on your hands. If the copy is riddled with *stets*, give in to the more harmless ones; that is, undo editing made for the sake of eloquence rather than correctness. You did your job—and you have the evidence in your tracked

---

2. In contrast, one of my favorite writer comments ever was written in the margin next to a change I'd made to fix an unfortunate turn in tone of voice: "WOOF! Yes. Gag, retch, vomit." I took that as approval.

changes and e-mails if you should need it. After you restore everything you possibly can, you will have to write a follow-up letter or e-mail in order to resolve the remaining loose ends. Use tact. Include some positive reactions. Thank the writer for his promptness or attention to detail. Apologize for anything boneheaded you did that caused trouble: "I'm sorry I misunderstood your win-loss statistics; I wish now I had asked you first. Thank you for sorting me out." Short of resorting to spinelessness, be generous in taking responsibility for awkward situations.[3] If you can, say that you think the work is now in much better shape as a result of his second pass.

One sign that you're dealing with a bully is when you receive an unhelpful answer to a polite or tentative question. You might have spotted something garbled that only the writer could untangle, and you wrote something like "Words missing here?" or "Is this what you intended?" with the confidence that the writer would see the problem and sort it out. But the bully simply wrote "No" or "Yes," and the problem remains. If you don't get another round with the writer in order to explain your initial query, that's the end of it. It might have helped to be more specific ("Are you referring to social networking sites?" Or "Change to 'social networking sites'?"). Another tactic is not to ask at all, but to simply barge ahead and make changes, drawing attention to what you've done and why:

—p. 34, para. 2: I changed "bludgeon" to "bludgeoned" for agreement.
—p. 54, line 4: I cut the third use of "ornery cuss" within two pages.

3. My manuscript editor just inserted a comment here: "One thing this job has taught me is how to apologize for things that aren't my fault!"

The hope is that by not asking, you don't invite a response; and if you got it wrong, in seeing how you misread it, the writer will understand the problem, fear that other senseless twits will also stumble, and fix it instead of writing *stet*.

If there are global issues that you consider nonnegotiable, register your intent to override the writer's *stets* without inviting a debate on each one. ("I restored most of the commas as you requested. In places where they separated complete sentences, however, I retained the semicolons or periods, with a few exceptions. If you feel strongly about this, we can discuss it.") If there are places where the writer seems to have rejected your editing without understanding the problem, spell it out. ("We don't want readers—or worse, reviewers—to take your wording as sexist.")

Depending on where you are in the editing and production process, you might drop an issue momentarily but return to it in your next communication. ("About that 'preface': I think we should add a line to your introduction explaining why you put it at the back of the book.") If the writer won't budge, you'll have to show more firmness and determination, but as long as you can, leave him some room to make the decision himself. ("Hello—just thought I'd let you know that I'm ready to submit this to production as soon as we resolve the preface issue. Any more thoughts on that?")

I have found that self-deprecation and humor have their place in dealing with difficult authors, but unless you are very sure of how your idea of humor will be received, it might be better to resist.[4] Some writers respond well to gentle teasing

---

4. In my experience, most writers, like most people, have a funny bone, even if you wouldn't guess it from their prose. I suspect that one of my writers left this in just to see if I would catch it: "At a South Side bar, they shoot each foreigner passing through the doorway cold, appraising looks."

about their foibles, perhaps enjoying the self-image as creative geniuses who can't be bothered with details. ("Your abbreviations in this section were—forgive me—eccentric. I hope you don't mind that I swept through and standardized them.")

Be especially cautious when you are tempted to use humor as an antidote to bad news. I once wrote to tell an author that the designer, production manager, and I had decided we could make only two of three changes she had requested very late in the publication process. In my e-mail, I breezily promised that we would make the third correction at the time of the first reprinting and went on to tell her about something funny that had happened to me since our last communication. I thought I knew the woman well enough, having worked on this project with her for over two years. Not only was she distressed that we wouldn't make the third correction, but she copied several people on her reply to me—which included the goofy story I'd sent her. In that case my attempt at humor not only misfired with the author; it also embarrassed me in front of my colleagues. (As for her forwarding of my note, that's an issue I'll visit later when I talk about e-mail management.)

Finally, if you are able to contact a writer by phone, consider doing so the minute you perceive difficulty. Not everyone is good at this. I'm not. But if you're good on the phone, it's a potential way to make friends with a writer who seems difficult on paper. Schedule the call by e-mail, so you're both prepared. Keep your conversation general, with several goals in mind. First, start with the assumption that the writer will respond to friendly professionalism; second, show that you're a reasonable person who takes the project seriously; and third, show that you don't need to have control over everything. Thank the writer for something—anything—and say something complimentary about the work. Give her a choice in a matter that you have little stake in, such as "How would you prefer we deal with the last few loose ends? Should I list them in an e-mail later this week, or would you rather see the entire document again?" If you are sincere and your tone is collaborative, the sound of your voice will remind the writer that you're a person, which might help temper her future responses. Just as likely, you'll learn that a writer whose written comments sounded cranky is actually a jolly curmudgeon whom you've misjudged. Important: take notes on the conversation, including the date, and follow up with a pleasant thank-you e-mail summarizing the outcome.

The beauty of these strategies is that they offer the writer a second chance to accept your decisions without further discussion. Sometimes difficult writers are defensive because they don't see or understand the issues, or they aren't conversant in grammar, or style changes alarm them. They lack the confidence or ability to explain or defend themselves, and when you push a little, they back down. Even if that's not the case, by stating your arguments you'll either get your way or you'll have an explicit objection from the author for the record.

PICKING YOUR BATTLES

Since we've already agreed that there's no room for power-tripping as a copy editor, it stands to reason that there are going to be times when it's expedient to back down. Every editor feels strongly about certain issues, but it's good to reexamine the reasons behind those feelings when they get in the way of progress. Ask yourself whether you're pushing a rule simply because it's a rule; ask whether the rule serves the text and the reader in this case.

When your writer is looking for reasons to be annoyed, shrug off minor style issues, concentrate on problems that hinder logic or clarity, and save your stubbornness for the offensive or illegal.

APPEALING TO AUTHORITY

You aren't alone, you know. When you find yourself debating an issue with a writer (or better yet, before it comes to that), use the tools at your elbow. While you are working on copy, justify editing decisions that you sense will mystify or annoy the writer, especially if you can tell from the writer's habits that your editing might seem inconsistent to him. Comments or in-text notes can clarify ("Pope Benedict; the pope; per *CMOS* 8.25"). Please don't do this more than very occasionally—you aren't being paid to document and defend your every move, and, paradoxically, you will damage your credibility if you feel compelled to do so, by seeming to lack confidence in your own knowledge and judgment. Instead, do it a couple of times near the beginning of a project and coast on the impression it gives: that you know what you're doing and you rely on authority. Once you show that you know your sources, it's understood; you needn't keep expressing them. ("I'll spell out numbers up to a hundred hereafter, with some exceptions for 'regional consistency.'") If you make a habit of enclosing a copy of your style sheet with the edited document, you can save yourself many explanations; the entries will do that work: "middle-class (adj.); middle class (n.)."

If an appeal to published sources doesn't win the day, you can always turn to human resources. At the risk of sounding all lemons-into-lemonady, I'll revisit one of the advantages of the humble status of the copy editor: there is almost always someone we can turn to when we need help with an unreasonable writer. It's not something you want to do regularly. Supervising editors don't have time for high-maintenance copy editors and will tend to look elsewhere if you can't fend for yourself. But they are all used to occasional appeals for help, and it's part of their job to intervene on your behalf when necessary. (My first managing editor and mentor at Chicago, the great Margaret Mahan, was once so exasperated by an author who complained unreasonably about one of her editors that she told him he was full of shit—although, in hindsight, she does not recommend that approach.)

Finally, remember that sometimes you get the last word. True, the writer gets the byline, but it's not the author's right to offend or confuse the reader, defy the rules of English, fail to identify sources, or lower the standards of your institution. It's likely that his contract says something to the effect that the publisher is allowed to make final editorial decisions in nonsubstantive style matters. Still, don't sneak: it's not fair simply to settle things your own way without notifying the writer. ("I've made all the corrections we agreed on, but I'm afraid that without a source or explanation for the Cheney quotation, I was forced to go with the paraphrased version we discussed.") Most authors won't sue.

A | In formal writing, we allow both a question mark and an exclamation mark only in the event that the author was being physically assaulted while writing. Otherwise, no.

CHAPTER FIVE

The Misguided Martyr

OR, LAYING DOWN YOUR LIFE
FOR THE SERIAL COMMA

Q | About two spaces after a period. As a US Marine, I know that what's right is right and you are wrong. I declare it once and for all aesthetically more appealing to have two spaces after a period. If you refuse to alter your bullheadedness, I will petition the commandant to allow me to take one Marine detail to conquer your organization and impose my rule. Thou shalt place two spaces after a period. Period. *Semper Fidelis.*

THE CORRECTORS

The fixation that copy editors have on "correctness" is unbounded, as the mail to the "Chicago Style Q&A" attests:

Q | Which is correct: "Find out who is the head of your division" or "Find out who the head of your division is"?
Q | Can we start sentences with *because*? I have grown up learning the slogan "We cannot start a sentence with *because*, because *because* is a conjunction."
Q | I have come across a construction that I am not used to at work: "We are focused against." I had been accustomed to

saying "focused on." Can you please tell me which of these is correct?[1]

When did we get the idea that English is so rigid a language that there is only one correct way to say something? Or the idea that consistency is mandatory or even desirable down to the minutest level of expression? Letters to the Q&A demonstrate a mania for correctness and consistency that, if applied universally, would give every piece of writing the same drab, expressionless, and mechanical style of prose.

ASSERTIONISM

It's impossible to frequent language and grammar websites and not be aware of the age-old battle between "prescriptivist" and "descriptivist" grammar linguists. At cartoonish extremes, the former are accused of defending a system of arbitrary, inflexible rules of English ("If it appeared in a grammar book anywhere at any time, it's a rule"), and the latter are said to promote a promiscuous and ever-changing collection of real-life slang ("If someone talks that way, it's correct"). Neither description is accurate or helpful. While grammarians and linguists vary in their views on what's correct or standard, and they may claim prescriptivist or descriptivist leanings, both sides have been known to do their homework and back up their views with historical evidence, analysis, and examples

---

1. Who is the head, or who the head is? Both are just fine. Begin a sentence with *because*? Yes: it's standard, classic, perfectly pedigreed English grammar. Focused against? Preposition choice varies. *Against* might not be the most common idiom, but is it wrong? Is it a regionalism? Did you look it up? Are you actually going to change it before you can answer those questions?

from literature and speech. And most understand that there are degrees of appropriateness: that the formal English in a book printed by a scholarly press would not necessarily be appropriate in a blog post or poem. They recognize not only that it would be ludicrous to impose a single form of English on all writers and speakers but that such restrictions would impoverish rather than enhance the language.

"Assertionists," on the other hand, do not agree. Law professor Eugene Volokh coined this term "for people who don't just say that prescriptions set forth by some supposed authorities define what is 'right' in English, but who simply assert a prescription even in the face of what those supposed authorities say."[2]

Assertionists take pride in rigid thinking. A good example is the style rule that legislates a comma before *and* in a series: lions, tigers[,?] and bears. Chicago favors the comma; AP discourages it. But just look up "serial comma" (or "Oxford comma" or "Harvard comma") online to find example after example of witless, raging allegiance to one style or the other with no acknowledgment that neither style can be used exclusively without occasionally resulting in nonsense or confusion.[3]

The sad fact is, in spite of their enthusiasm for imposing rules on other people's copy, copy editors are not always aware that some of their long-held rules are controversial or have even been discarded. In many of the questions to the Q&A, askers are tormented by what they see as declining standards in print. They write, "I see this error more and more in print," or "This isn't what I was taught," or "When did this rule change?"

Getting hung up on phantom issues and personal bugaboos

2. Eugene Volokh, "Descriptivism, Prescriptivism, and Assertionism," *The Volokh Conspiracy* blog, October 4, 2011, http://volokh.com/2011/10/04/descriptivism-prescriptivism-and-assertionism/.
3. Famous examples: "This book is dedicated to my parents, Ayn Rand and God," and "She invited her father, Mitt Romney, and the pope."

can affect the actual editing in negative ways beyond slowing it down to write indignant letters to *The Chicago Manual of Style*. First, in your zeal to ferret out every last *which* and change it to *that* (because you mistakenly believe that it's important in every case), you are likely to overlook potentially more serious problems. You may have noticed this phenomenon: often it seems that the more tinkering you do in a document, the more errors remain. The writer will point out an error you missed while editing, and you can hardly believe it got by you. Then you notice that in the preceding sentence, you had twice replaced *due to* with *because of*. Flush from that Pyrrhic victory, you had sailed right past the dangling participle.

Second, in covering the page with unnecessary and counterproductive little edits, you will irritate the writer and demonstrate the shallowness of your editorial judgment. And when a writer begins to believe that his editor is incompetent, his natural response is to start putting things back the way they were. All at once you're adversaries—and all the good work you did becomes a baby in the bathwater.

Which brings us back to the issue of knowing your stuff. When was the last time you looked at a recently published book on grammar and usage, rather than the one you used in school or on your first job? When you're deciding to go to the mat over your favorite authorial transgressions, reconsider. Can you find justification in more than one respected source? (Mrs. Hangstrup's 1980 lecture on not ending sentences with prepositions doesn't count.) If my questions make you uneasy, keep reading.[4]

---

4. I like Arthur Plotnik's point about unthinkingly disallowing the passive voice: "A little Strunk and White is a dangerous thing. Some editors are driven by a cursory reading of *The Elements of Style* to

SKUNKED RULES

Sometimes it doesn't matter whether a rule we learned has long been out of style among the cognoscenti; if we think our readers will call it an error, we don't want to allow it. Although style and grammar rules change and acceptance levels change, the problem is knowing how to judge whether a usage or construction has become acceptable to our expected audience. After all, editors need to be conservative. It's not good for business to be on the cutting edge of grammar.

And that's where continuing education comes in. In order to feel confident about our choices, we need to *read*. It's important for editors to know that linguists and language experts are not only not outraged by the singular *they*, but in many cases recommend it—whether you agree or not. So where do you learn about language and writing trends? Books on language are fun and helpful, but they can be outdated by the time they're printed. The answer is that you have to read online, and social media is essential for keeping up. More on that later.

FOOLISH CONSISTENCIES

Don't ever tell a copy editor that consistency is the hobgoblin of little minds. To begin with, anyone who knows the actual wording of that chestnut ("a foolish consistency") knows that

---

change such sentences as 'the outcry was heard round the world' to 'everyone in the world heard the outcry.'" Arthur Plotnik, *The Elements of Editing: A Modern Guide for Editors and Journalists* (New York: Collier/Macmillan, 1982), 3–4.

Emerson wasn't thinking about whether *website* needs a hyphen, and, second, most of the mismatches we correct are not foolish. What's more, whatever the stereotype, good copy editors do draw a line when it comes to consistency.

Because inconsistencies can distract, confuse, or inconvenience readers, eliminating them is one of the primary goals of editing. We look for gaffes such as the following:

- midsentence change in tense
- same-level headings styled differently
- words spelled more than one way
- changes in alphabetizing method
- multiple abbreviations for the same term

On the other hand, there are situations where consistency is optional or even misguided. Some are undisputed: no one is tempted for the sake of consistency to spell out all numbers no matter how large or complex, or to use a person's full name upon every mention no matter how frequent. But here are just a few examples of inconsistencies I recently had to argue in favor of:

- comma before *or*, *and*, or *because*
- tenses of verbs introducing quotations (Aristotle says, Ringo wrote)
- punctuation of different lists within a document
- commas versus colons introducing quoted matter
- citation styles in the notes versus those in the text
- capped or lowercased letter beginning a quotation

The next time you think you are on a campaign for consistency and correctness, just remember that it is always wrong to make corrections robotically without considering whether each change is an actual improvement. "Regional consistencies"—that is, when clashing styles within eyeshot of each other are forced to conform, causing one of them to break style—are often the more practical goal. Harrowing through a manuscript to add a comma before every *too*? Let's leave that to the hobgoblins.

RULES ARE MADE TO BE BROKEN; COPY EDITORS ARE NOT

Copy editors often ask questions that leave me scratching my head. But the ones that flummox me the most amount to something like this: "If I follow all the rules in this case, nonsense and chaos will result. What should I do?"

What is it about American culture—or education, or religion, or parenting—that prevents an otherwise normal, intelligent person from concluding without my help that in cases like this *you should break a rule*?

A researcher writing endnotes wonders about including the name of the state in the place of publication in addition to the city. His style guide says not to add the state name if it's obvious from the name of the publisher, such as the University of Virginia Press (rule 1). But then, in order to impose consistency (rule 2), he must leave out *all* state names, with the result that readers will assume that a book published in London, Ohio, was published in the UK. What to do?

An editor working on a bibliography encounters a source who signs all work with an initial instead of a full first name. The rest of the bibliography includes full names. The style manual says to use full names. And then there's that consistency thing. What should she do? Well, I want to reply, what are our choices here? Make up a name? Delete that source? Change all 437 author names to initials only? Why do they have to ask?

I'll tell you why: it's because for many writers and editors, our work is all about the rules. It's what we do—we take a chunk of writing and we grind it through the style-guide mill, and we never once stop to ask whether logic and reason and the *reader* are served. The first question is always "What's the rule?" instead of "What is helpful?" or "What makes sense?" or—the unthinkable—"Can I break this rule?"

We have the power to break the rule.

Of course it's fine for "What's the rule?" to be the first question—as long as it's not the only question. After all, an understanding of the rules is our best tool for getting writers out of tight spots. And note that I said an *understanding* of the rules, which is not the same as an ability to recite them. Understanding the thinking behind a style choice gives you the power both to discard it when better thinking should prevail and to argue for it more convincingly when the reasoning applies.

I recently spoke to a classroom of new copy editors, and I took this "knowledge is power" idea one step further. Copy editors have a choice as to what kind of power they wield. They can wave the rule book about and try to assume the power of saying "No, you can't" to writers, or they can acquire the power of knowing when to break a rule in order to help writers achieve great writing.

You know by now that I like to call that second choice "subversive," but I hope you're also getting the idea that it truly isn't. Choose the second kind of power: it's a better way of life.

USING YOUR HEAD

Q | The guidance given in *CMOS* 10.3 states that when using abbreviations, "the terms must be spelled out on their first occurrence." Does spelling it out in a footnote or a figure caption, which is the first occurrence, mean that it does not need to be spelled out the first time it appears in the body of the document?

Q | When using an author's name in the text, i.e., "John Smith says . . . ," is the full name (first and last) used, as in my example, or just the last name?

The first question above is a good question. The asker wants to follow a rule (and "must be spelled out on their first occurrence" certainly reads as a firm rule), but the rule isn't clear: does occurrence in a footnote or figure caption, which might be in small type or on another page, count as "first occurrence," or must the first mention appear in the main body of the document?

The problem is that (1) the asker has not thought about the reasoning behind the guidance, and (2) she is concerned with technicalities, rather than with helping the reader.

If she were to think for only a few seconds about *why* an unfamiliar abbreviation should be spelled out on first occurrence rather than later on, I have no doubt that she could come up with the obvious reason: that delaying the explanation would mystify and frustrate the reader. Knowing what the goal is—to make sure the reader isn't inconvenienced by an unfamiliar abbreviation—it's easy to make a decision to add the explanation wherever the reader might light upon it first, even if it means doing it twice.

The second question is, frankly, the kind that makes me despair, although I always try to allow for the possibility that it doesn't tell the whole story of what prompted the writer to ask. Even so, it's hard to imagine why he didn't try a little harder to think this through: "Would a rule outlawing the use of an author's surname—or requiring it on every mention—be reasonable?" or "Haven't I seen full names followed by shortened names my entire reading life?" I'm confident the asker had the resources to solve the question—he had the resources to write to *CMOS*. But he simply didn't use his head.

Being superfocused on following the rules can cause us to lose sight of what's important and what's trivial in producing a clear and readable document. When writers and editors don't think for themselves, they must repeatedly resort to searching for someone who will tell them what to do. This pernicious habit stunts learning, wastes time, and does little to benefit the reader.

That said, it's undeniable that editors legitimately spend a great deal of their time looking things up. There's plenty we don't know—there's no shame in that—and there are many times when we need information in order to edit intelligently. Which leads to my next point: efficient editors know how to find things out.

LOOKING IT UP

Few things are as annoying as not being able to find something. But at least in most cases we know what we're looking for—keys, dog, car—and we're pretty sure it exists.

Searching for a style or grammar rule can be tougher. We

don't always know whether there actually is one, much less what it's called, and those are serious impediments to figuring out where it might be hiding. In years of reading questions e-mailed to the Chicago Q&A, I've surmised a few reasons why the askers couldn't find a rule.

They hadn't actually looked. Like children whining that they can't find their socks, they write, "How do you make *USA Today* plural: I bought two *USA Todays?* I've looked everywhere and I can't find how to make the plural of a word in italics." When I'm feeling patient, I explain how to type "plural italics" into the search box or look in the index under "italics: plurals of words in" or "plurals: words or phrases in italics."[5]

They didn't know what to look for. This I understand, because it regularly happens to me. Is it *who* or *whom* in "I wanted to speak with who(m)ever stole the Twinkie"? What's the name of this grammar issue? What words would you look under in a reference book to read about it? (Never fear—we'll know by the end of the chapter.)

The rule doesn't exist. When I've tried everything and come up dry, I begin to fear that I'm obsessing over something everyone knows but me, a rule so obvious and basic that it goes without saying. I have to remind myself that it's more likely that there simply is no rule. I wish I had a list of all the alleged rules we've been asked to confirm at the Q&A. Like the one that says you can't have an illustration in a preface. Or that "said Julie" must always be changed to "Julie said."

Copy editors, as opposed to the general reader, often have

---

5. *CMOS*, 16th ed., 7.11: "If italicized terms—names of newspapers, titles of books, and the like—are used in the plural, the *s* is normally set in roman. A title already in plural form, however, may be left unchanged. In case of doubt, avoid the plural by rephrasing."

the advantage of knowing how to do basic research, but they have the disadvantage of overconfidence. They simply barge ahead without checking, writing time-wasting queries to authors like these:

—p. 6, para. 3: Are "emic" and "etic" meant as suffixes? Add hyphens, as in "-emic" and "-etic"?[6]

—p. 8, line 1: Is there a word missing after "obtains"?[7]

—p. 9, para. 2: About the phrase "a red herring drawn across the historian's trail?"—can a herring be drawn across a trail?[8]

By now, I have a great deal of experience in looking things up, so I'm here to testify: like all skills, it gets easier with practice. Here are some ways to find grammar and style rules when you aren't sure what you're looking for.

Consult an up-to-date dictionary or usage manual. Dictionaries aren't just for definitions. Many of us (e.g., me), scrape by on grammatical intuition, without being well educated in its lingo. The examples in a good dictionary are useful for putting names to vague notions, such as whether *as* in a given sentence is an adverb, a pronoun, or a preposition. The usage notes and discussions, sometimes extensive, settle many popular debates—for instance, that it's fine to use *since* to mean *because*, and for how many centuries that's been so. Even if you don't find the answer you're seeking, the labels and terms found in the definitions and examples will almost always help

---

6. *Emic* and *etic* are anthropology terms, not suffixes.

7. *Obtains* can be intransitive.

8. From *Merriam-Webster's Collegiate Dictionary* (11th ed.), s.v. "red herring": "from the practice of drawing a red herring across a trail to confuse hunting dogs . . . : something that distracts attention from the real issue."

you search elsewhere. A usage manual like *Garner's Modern American Usage* offers cross-references to aid navigation (e.g., "*mode of operandi. See modus operandi*").

Search online. When I don't know the grammar for what I'm seeking, I'm amazed at how often I can learn it by simply typing related words into a search engine. To find an answer to the "I wanted to speak with who(m)ever stole the Twinkie" question, I Googled "whoever or whomever." A quick scan down the list of results took me to a post at a site I knew and had some confidence in, which explained that in constructions like this, *whoever* is correct, because it is the subject of *stole*, not the object of the preposition *with*.[9] Even if your first results don't take you to an answer, they are likely to contain some terms that will help you refine your search.

Once you know what you're looking for, you can go directly to an online grammar or style site or forum. You can easily find them by typing "online grammar" into a search engine. University websites are a good place to start. The University of Chicago Writing Program has a page of suggestions, and one site will typically lead you to others. (Note that some forums are open only to members or subscribers.)

Ask a friend. Here at work, I'm lucky to have a platoon of savvy colleagues and a company culture that allows me to appear in someone's doorway and say, "I can't remember this grammar thing, and I don't know what it's called, but it's whether the whatever goes before or after the other thing," and the person will say "Oh, yeah—it goes before." A grammar pal

---

9. The object of *with* is the noun clause "whoever stole the Twinkie." Neal Whitman, "Whoever or Whomever: Learn the Rule (or How to Avoid the Issue)," *Quick and Dirty Tips* blog, June 18, 2011, accessed April 19, 2015, http://www.quickanddirtytips.com/education/grammar/whoever-or-whomever?page=1.

for mutual aid and debate should be on every editor's list of must-have resources.

A | As a US Marine, you're probably an expert at something, but I'm afraid it's not this. *Status quo.*

CHAPTER SIX

Dear Writers

A CHAPTER OF YOUR OWN

Q | I read a lot and have been working on a novel of my own
for a while now. In most of the materials I read, the authors
use "had had" and "that that" quite often. For example: "He
had had the dog for twelve years and everyone knew that that
was the real reason he didn't want Animal Control to take it."
I doubt there is any actual rule against this, but I find it to be
unattractive on a purely aesthetic basis and try to avoid it like
the plague when writing. Is there anything to this or am I just
weird?

A chapter for writers was not in the original plan for this book.
Some copy editors might even feel that our secret and subversive club won't seem authentic without a "No Writers Allowed"
sign tacked up on the tree house. But while I was working on
the book, I was surprised more than once when writer friends
said they wanted to read it. I assured them that what they
wanted to read was a book written by acquiring editors or developmental editors—not copy editors.[1] And they told me I
was wrong.

1. Acquiring editors are the ones who scout out work and contract it
for a publisher. If a project isn't yet in publishable form, an ac-

Writers, understandably, have mixed feelings about having their work copyedited, and they are curious and sometimes nervous about the process. They would like to know what they can do to prepare for it and what to do if they disagree with the changes. And since one of the main points of this book is to welcome writers into our club (and since, as a writer, I sometimes sit on the other side of the desk myself), it seems right to think about things from the author's point of view.

ACTS OF SUBMISSION

Occasionally a writer handing in work will suggest skipping the copyediting stage, offering assurance that the work has already been read several times. Some of my authors have noted that they even paid for freelance editing before submitting their work. Although it is true that some manuscripts are in excellent shape, in my experience the likelihood that a given project will need no editing bears little relation to the number of times it has been vetted by colleagues, employees, or children of the writer. I would go further and venture that if I were to pluck any published book or magazine article from the library shelf and have it scanned into typescript format for editing, most copy editors would still find a fair bit to meddle with.

How can this be?

First, the habits and standards and style manuals of publishers vary. Even more to the point, the preferences and knowl-

---

quisitions editor might help the writer develop it, either before or after it's under contract. Or he might turn it over to a developmental editor, who will analyze the project and work with the writer to pull it into publishable shape. Both types of editors might do some copyediting while they're at it, but it's likely to be random and inconsistent because they are concerned with larger issues. They assume a copy editor will go over the piece later.

edge of copy editors vary. A lot. Comma choice alone leaves so much room for discretion that it would be nearly impossible for two editors working independently to punctuate a work of some length in the same way. A certain amount of editing is optional and subjective. What one editor considers acceptable is incorrect to another. One reads with his eyes, another with her ears, and they edit accordingly. Some concentrate on logic and flow; some are sticklers for grammar; and some, like an indulgent mother with a sticky toddler, let everything but the most obvious and egregious messes slide by.

Even if all editors were of the same sensibility and training, editing is by nature multitasking, reading at several levels simultaneously—in fact, it's common for editors to read more than once, concentrating on big-picture issues in one reading, details in another. Inevitably, we are distracted as we read by the issues that interest us the most, and inevitably we overlook or dismiss some matters as unworthy of attention.

My point is that a work will never be edited the same way twice, and it will never be considered perfect, no matter how many times it's edited—probably not even by the last person who edited it. (An assigning editor at a famous children's magazine told me of her exasperation after one of her staff had copyedited the same text in three revisions and kept finding errors. "Stop looking for mistakes!" she yelled. "Think like an editor and just let it go!")

The second reason that copy must undergo copyediting regardless of its state at submission is that it must be prepared for typesetting. Although a writer under contract is usually given guidelines for formatting and organizing her work, it's the rare author who follows the guidelines closely. A certain amount of the copy editor's time must be spent in removing pretty font and type styles, redoing weirdly typed block quotations (the kind with tabs at the beginning of every line), and cleaning up whatever else the writer did while trying to be helpful in spite of the guidelines. Writers are endlessly inventive when it comes to word processing. In the early days of personal computing, a colleague showed me a book manuscript that consisted of 350 Microsoft Word documents; the author had started a new file each time he reached the bottom of a page. Today, citation builders are the copy editor's nemesis. Although their potential is thrilling, very few writers know how to use them; the result is more often than not a perfect—though consistent!—mess. But even if writers were to follow every instruction, guidelines for writers aren't intended to produce a production-ready document; they merely eliminate part of the cleanup.

So when you submit work—even if it consists of previously published material—be prepared for someone to find something that needs changing. When we talk about not taking editing "personally," realize that this is why. A good amount of copyediting has nothing to do with how great a writer you are.

If you work in a specialized area or with unconventional content, prepare to be edited by someone who is not an expert in that area—or a mind reader. If you're lucky, she will have experience editing related books or articles, but if she hasn't, she will welcome a page from you with explanations and preferences. (For example, "The term *improvisative* should not be corrected to *improvisational* or *improvisatory*"; or "Please don't change the spellings of place-names without asking; it's a political issue.")

Whenever you are about to be edited, feel free to ask questions about who will edit your work, what kinds of things they'll be looking for, and how much feedback and negotiation to expect. If you have fears or concerns (other than "Incompetent editors terrify me"), expressing them up front might make a difference in the approach your editor takes.

In light of all this, is it worth the time and money to hire a copy editor in advance of submitting your work? That depends. On the one hand, if you feel that your writing is in pretty good shape, there's little point in paying someone to copyedit to a particular style only to have your publisher redo it to a different one. On the other hand, if your readers have been marking a lot of typos and writing "huh?" in the margins here and there, your work might benefit from a pass specifically addressing those kinds of issues.

There are other good reasons to get professional editorial help before submission. If you are required to identify sources and you aren't confident that your notes and references are complete and conform to one of the commonly accepted styles (Chicago, MLA, APA, etc.), a copy editor can put things right. If you are trying to break into a field of writing and your work is being done on speculation, small sloppinesses can land your work in the rejection pile. An editorial eye will spy the remaining flaws.

WHY YOU ARE NOT A TYPESETTER

Word processors are wondrously fun to play with, and writers who secretly believe they have a talent for graphic design seem unable to resist availing themselves of every bell and whistle.

That's fine if you're self-publishing. But otherwise, formatting to this degree is not only unhelpful, it's even a little dangerous—and not just because it's a sure way to tire your copy editor before she reads a word of your text.

Maybe you feel you're helping by sharing your vision for the design of your work. But a publisher, editor, or designer who may be in awe of your literary or intellectual talent has considerably less interest in your vision for design. That's what *they* do. And to do it, they will have to undo all your efforts.

Although it might seem easy to clear formatting with a click, a copy editor would be rash to do that. Rather, he will have to consider whether each instance of bold, italics, or small caps serves a purpose and should be preserved.

There are two basic methods for restoring simplicity to a tarted-up text, neither of which a writer likes to imagine: (1) like generations of wallpaper, your fancy accretions can be scraped away a layer at a time, or (2) like a condemned hovel, they can be bulldozed and rebuilt from scratch. Neither method is foolproof; both risk violence to the content.

To safeguard your text and endear yourself to your publishing team, follow these fundamental rules when you prepare your document (but be sure to check the submission guidelines of your publisher—they will trump any suggestions of mine):

- Ask what application your files may be submitted in.
- Use a standard serif type like Times New Roman. If you need special characters in a special font, ask for advice on how best to submit them.
- Ask whether it's OK to include automated list numbering, field codes, live hyperlinks, or anything that moves or flashes. You might have to eliminate them or convert them to plain typing before submitting your work.
- Turn off the hyphenation feature of your word processor.
- Leave the right-hand margin ragged, not justified, in order to avoid   giant   spaces   between   words.

· Indent new paragraphs instead of putting space between paragraphs. Editors need to see indention for various reasons, even if the final design doesn't feature indents.

Keeping your document clean and simple will help to ensure that it appears in type the way you intended. A nice side benefit is that your copy editor will love you for it.

TIPS FOR SELF-EDITING

Reading your own work objectively is a trick that some master more easily than others. The best-known tactic is highly effective: put your writing away for as long as you're able, and then read it with a fresh eye. Unfortunately, that trick is available only to those who work ahead, have no deadlines, or conduct research in fields that change slowly. Most writers don't have the luxury of putting their work in a drawer for a month.

As a copy editor, I've noticed some glitches that writers often fail to see in their own work, as well as a few imagined flaws that they appear to monitor needlessly.

Things writers miss:

· *Throat-clearing.* Writer Richard Peck claims that when he finishes a novel, he throws out the first chapter without reading it and writes it anew. He reasons that when we begin a work, we're rarely certain of where it will end. Revisiting the beginning after the end has emerged makes sense. This time it will be easier to eliminate unneeded windup verbiage.
· *Personal tics.* Most writers have a few pet words or phrases: *decidedly*, or *by no means*, or *incredibly*, or *most important*.

Ditto for favorite sentence constructions: "Not only X but Y" is popular. Once you identify your own foibles, they become more difficult to ignore.

· *Repetition.* Word processing encourages this to the same degree that old-fashioned typewriting discouraged it: why say something once when you can say it three times? A common keyboard error is to *copy* and paste when you mean to *cut* and paste, so that whole passages are accidentally repeated verbatim.

· *Non sequiturs.* Although these can occur with no help from technology, they are another by-product of sloppy word processing. When text gets moved around, new transitions are sometimes needed to connect the dots.

Conversely, a number of so-called rules are obediently observed by writers who haven't cracked a grammar guide since high school. As a result, the writers avoid a raft of constructions that are actually just fine:

Things writers "correct" needlessly:

· *The passive voice.* When it doesn't obscure, mislead, or intrude, judicious use of the passive is a needed and honorable feature of fluent formal English.

· *The first person.* Even formal scholarly writing came around some time ago to allowing a writer to speak for himself.

· *Split infinitives.* And prepositions at the ends of sentences. And sentences beginning with *and* or *but*. And sentence fragments. These prohibitions and quite a few more are long-discredited shibboleths.

Although I suppose I could write myself out of a job by posting the secrets of self-editing, I'm not seriously worried.

Rather, if writers were better able to clean up their work at the basic level, copy editors would be free to concentrate on polishing, their productivity would increase, and the finished work would benefit.

ARE YOU A DIFFICULT WRITER?

Difficult writers and difficult people tend to share some characteristics; you might already know whether you are one or not. If you feel that being difficult is something you do well and rather enjoy, then carry on. Otherwise, consider this bit of self-examination and amateur therapy.

Granted, difficult writers are often good writers. Reasonably protective of their prose, they unreasonably see editing as an assault.

- They are defensive. They read the editing with "No" at the ready. Unwilling to consider why a particular change might be helpful, and unable to read objectively to find the problem in the original, they assume that they know best and that the editor is meddling.
- They are uncommunicative and dictatorial, writing *Stet* or *No* everywhere and never engaging in dialogue or negotiation with the editor.
- They are unobservant. In a figure caption, they object to the editor's lowercasing of *Classical*, never mind the consistent use of *classical* everywhere else in the work.
- They excessively second-guess the editing and challenge perceived inconsistencies and minor style issues.
- They are passive-aggressive or rude. Where the copy editor failed to catch an instance of something she has been chang-

ing throughout, instead of simply marking it or querying, they force a confession of incompetence: "I fail to see how this is different from the examples you changed in paragraphs 1 and 3."

- They inflate the value of their own outdated knowledge of grammar and style, and they misjudge their consistency in applying it to their own writing.
- They don't understand writing and publishing technology, and they get upset when they're forced to accommodate it.
- They fail to read cover letters or follow directions or notify their editors of delays.
- They are outraged by any imperfection in the finished project.

The point of submitting a piece of writing to the scrutiny of another is that self-editing is so darned hard. Writers need another set of eyes on their work because they compose at a high level of abstraction and detail. Few brains can simultaneously monitor conceptual progress and mechanical detail without lapses. Academic copy editors find plenty to improve even in the writing of English professors—just as those professors are perfectly able to point out errors in writing other than their own.

Easy writers—most writers, in my experience—object in reasonable tones to editing that doesn't suit them, and they forgive an editor's occasional lapses or inability to understand specialist content. They are curious and open to learning about trends in style and grammar. They keep in touch regarding deadlines; they ask questions; they express appreciation. The best ones enjoy the dialogue, the banter, and the spirited arguments that are part of a true collaboration.

THE WAITING GAME

While your work is in copyediting—for a day, a week, or sometimes months—it might be difficult for you to keep your hands off it. That's understandable, and it's not a terrible thing, but there are two reasons why it would be better if you could let it rest, for now. First, there's a chance that you'll merely be duplicating work that your editor is doing, and you'll only waste her time by asking her to check a list of typos that she's already corrected. And second, your work will benefit from your gaining a little distance from it. You'll get a chance soon enough to read the entire thing again when the editing is sent for your approval, and if you've been away from it thinking about other things, you'll return to it with a fresh eye.

It's possible that even if you're trying not to think about your work, various corrections, additions, and little improvements will occur to you anyway. Just write them down so you can tend to them when it's your turn. Ask your copy editor whether she minds you e-mailing bits and pieces to her while she's working. I always appreciate having the information right away, so I can incorporate it while the style particular to that project is fully in my mind. Others would rather you make all your corrections later, at one time. Try to respect your editor's wishes.

Occasionally during the downtime, a writer finds that she's completely rethinking a major point—even to the extent of adding new text or an illustration or an appendix. It's the writer's responsibility to alert the copy editor of the new development the minute it becomes a real possibility. The copy editor can then decide whether the change in plan is serious enough to warrant running it by the boss, the assigning editor, the acquiring editor. If the new material will need expert review, the publisher might want to rethink the schedule, and the copy editor might be asked to put the project aside until everything is resolved. The magazine article will run in a later issue; the book will deliver in the fall instead of in the spring.

Something you should never do once editing has begun is to make changes to the original in the expectation that you can send it to the copy editor, who will somehow incorporate this new version into her work. By the time you send it, she will have spent time cleaning and coding and making countless silent changes to your files, so there's no way she will want to start over with your replacement file. Even if you tracked your changes, she will have to transfer each one to her working copy, tediously reediting, restyling, and recoding them. Of course, if the editor is feeling in control and professional, she will just suck it up and deal with the nuisance. After all, it's your work. You're her second master, next to the reader. She wants what you want.

But it's also possible that she won't be able to summon up that much professionalism and will instead lose all interest in your project.

(Just so you know.)

WHAT? WHERE? WHEN?

Three true stories:

> Writer A sends a panicky e-mail to her freelance copy editor (subject line URGENT MESSAGE!) reporting that she can't figure out how to accept or reject the tracked changes in the edited manuscript. The freelancer replies: "Yes, the files have

been locked on purpose, as I indicated in my cover note to you. We do not want you to accept or reject the changes. Here, again, are the instructions. . . ."

Writer B sends a huffy message complaining that he cannot find the footnotes in the edited manuscript I sent him. I reply that I took them out of his separate notes file and linked them individually to the callout numbers in the main text file, embedding them electronically. He replies with sarcasm that I might have told him. (From my cover letter: "I have embedded the footnotes electronically so they're tied to the corresponding location in the text. I'm noting it only so you won't be startled by it.")

Writers S through Z (I'll spare you C through R) respond reasonably to their page proofs—except for flat-out ignoring my instruction that added text be compensated for by cutting an equal amount of text nearby and vice versa. In some instances, they add whole paragraphs, perhaps expecting that the printer will simply tape a little flap into every book as it's printed.

You might see a theme developing here, something along the lines of "What's So Hard about Reading a Cover Letter?"

It's not as though a copy editor's instructions for reading galleys or proofs are arbitrary and frivolous. Although you may suspect that copy editors delight in ways to assert power over writers, requiring them to read a cover letter and follow the instructions is not one of them. Rather, the instructions tell you how to communicate your intentions precisely, not just to the editor but to the typesetter. Following them prevents expensive errors, delays, and charges for excessive alterations to proof.

My usual practice is to beg the writer to read the cover letter all the way through, "even if your eyes begin to glaze over," and I explain why this is important. But on the theory that the problem begins with casual arrogance on the part of the writer ("Who me? Take instruction from a copy editor? I could do this in my sleep!"), I'm wondering whether I might get better results if I simply wrote, "To avoid being billed for excessive typesetting charges, please use standard markings. Let me know if you need any help."

OK, that was a bit of a rant, for which I apologize. Whenever someone like me complains about writers, the result is a tsunami of complaints from writers about copy editors. I get a lot of good material that way. So go ahead and write your own book—and send me a copy!

WHY DEADLINES ARE DEADLINES

While you were in the process of writing, you may have had the luxury of dawdling. Once your book or article is in copyediting, the schedule becomes a much more real and serious part of the process, and one that you will have little control over—other than to cause delays when the ball is in your court. Although most writers are eager for their work to be published and will do everything they can to expedite the process, a surprising number are more casual about deadlines and seem to think nothing of racking up significant delays in the return of edited copy, page proofs, or indexes.

If you are writing for a periodical or any project with a short schedule, the deadlines will be pretty much set in stone and specified in your contract; a writer who procrastinates may simply be ignored while her project is either jettisoned or taken over by someone else. So ask ahead of time when you will be expected to be available to vet the editing or look at proofs, and if anything comes up that you think might interfere with the schedule, give reasonable warning. If your editor knows in advance about schedule conflicts, she might be able to re-shuffle things with typesetters and publicity contacts or move your work to another issue or season. Unexpected holdups will leave everyone in the lurch.

For longer-term projects like books, there are still good reasons to respect your publisher's schedule, and most of them directly benefit your project. Once a publisher makes a commitment to your book, every department—from editing and design to production and promotion—sets about creating the optimal conditions for its release. The schedule is a small miracle of coordination between departments, and a delay at any point can cause an equal delay in publication or, worse, will compound into catastrophe.

EDITING AS A GIFT, NOT AN INSULT

You know what it's like to come back to a hotel room in the afternoon and find that housekeeping has been there and everything is all fresh and put to rights? That's how a copy editor would like you to feel when you see the editing. If you can view extra-thorough editing as the mint on the pillow, all the better. What we don't want is for you to feel offended that we saw the need for cleaning.

If a copy editor has made a smart suggestion, brought clarity to a badly written passage, inspired you with a leading question, or pointed out a flaw in your argument, how are you going to react? I can guess your first thought: you will wish you had done it yourself. And almost every writer has been appalled at a boneheaded error that survived all the way to the copy editor. A magazine fact-checker told me of a celebrity puff piece in which the writer quoted an actor claiming to have hiked 5,723 miles up a mountain, and a profile in which another writer had absentmindedly typed the name of her tailor instead of the name of an actress's father. (The tailoring claim ticket had been tacked on the bulletin board in front of her while she typed.) The fact-checker spent hours trying to verify the connection.

Your second reaction will be to resent someone else's having done it (and a mere copy editor at that—go on, admit it), and your third impulse will be to wonder whether it's fair for you to accept what she did and present it as your own.

Of course it's fair. It's what we hope for. Nothing is more gratifying than for us to receive edited copy back from a writer with the editing for the most part intact. One of the nicest responses I've ever had from a writer was in the form of a paragraph he added to the end of his novel. I had admitted being a little disappointed by the ending even though it was the only sensible outcome. The rewrite addressed my feelings without changing the facts of the story. I couldn't have been more pleased.

We know that writers don't work in a vacuum and that before your work reaches us, it's been improved at many stages by the encouragement and critiquing of others. You've done the most difficult part, gathering the research, organizing, thinking, getting the words onto the page, revising in response to criticism. You've made it easy for us to read the finished product and pick at the little rough spots.

"*ILS ONT CHANGÉ MA CHANSON . . .*"

If all goes well, you'll be happy with the editing of your work. But what if you aren't? What if you start reading and right away you see that you've been terribly misunderstood? The copy editor has rewritten phrasings that are standard and necessary in your field. She removed a numbering system that she didn't realize was based on a related work. Where you chose not to define terms, she added glosses that your readers will find patronizing and juvenile. She struck through all the personal names that you transliterated according to the linguistic system you're celebrated for inventing and replaced them with spellings she found at *Wikipedia*.

Don't panic. Keep reading, and make notes. Everything that has been changed can be changed back, and you should assume that your copy editor will be willing to put back everything she got wrong. Your review is an opportunity for negotiation and improvement. The editor probably indicated as much in her cover letter. She is expecting to go another round. Small matters of style are most likely to be negotiable. A researcher and copy editor at one national magazine told me that after John Updike complained about the house spelling of *kidnaped* and *kidnaping*, the publisher changed the stylebook to Updike's preferred *kidnapped* and *kidnapping*. Even if you aren't John Updike, you still might get what you want if you ask.

Look at an offending edit and figure out why the editor thought the text needed help. Keep in mind that (a) you may be ignorant of your publisher's house style, and that (b) if you haven't consulted a grammar or style handbook for a few years, things change, and that (c) if the editor misunderstood you, other readers may too. If you don't like the editor's solution, figure out a better one and write it in. If you are convinced that the original wording is the way you want it, type *stet* beside it. And in those instances where you fear having to go another round on the issue with the editor, offer a brief explanation.

A caveat on "consistency": it is not always a goal. Sometimes it is optional or even misguided. For instance, it's normal to

- spell out and use numerals for the same number in different contexts;
- vary comma usage before *and* or *or* (He never drank gin or vodka or milk; he longed to adopt a pet—a dog, or a cat, or a squirrel);
- vary commas between repeated words (yada yada; big, big trouble);
- hyphenate phrases before a noun (a well-intentioned memo) but not after (the memo was well intentioned);
- cap a word in one place but lowercase it in another (Queen Elizabeth, the queen of England; the math department, the Department of Mathematics).

At Chicago's Q&A, writers frequently ask questions about consistency in terms of "always" or "never": Is *First Lady* always capitalized? Is it true that you should never put a comma after *yet*? But anyone who reads or writes for a living knows that there are always exceptions that depend on syntax, intentions, or audience. "Regional consistency" is an accepted editorial practice, whereby style rules are tweaked for the sake of minimizing unavoidable distractions to the reader.[2] In sum, it may

2. Regional consistency is one editorial solution when a style rule depends on context. For example, Chicago style omits hyphens after prefixes (*multiauthor*) but makes an exception for repeated vowels (*multi-institutional*). In a sentence where the same prefix would appear hyphenated in one word but closed up in another, it's acceptable or even advisable to break style for one of the words (*multi-author*).

save everyone some trouble if you discuss issues of perceived inconsistencies with your copy editor before "fixing" them on your own.

Although you might find yourself infuriated by what looks like clueless or incompetent editing, the second-worst thing you can do is explode in anger and rail at the copy editor. (The worst thing you can do is explode in anger and rail about her to her superiors.) Explain in the margins or in a cover letter why you believe that the editing was misguided. Although it might be difficult for you to rein in your exasperation, there's no point in humiliating and abusing the editor, and it will only make it more difficult to return to more cordial debate—especially if you are proven wrong. In short, although I can't deny that bad editing happens, there is almost always recourse. Start with the assumption that you can work things out, and you are more likely to get results.

Although your copy editor may be willing to restore almost everything you insist upon, it's usual for there to be a few matters she will want to discuss further. If there were places where you didn't respond or simply wrote *stet* without addressing the problem she was trying to fix, the problem will still be there. She may write back asking you to find a way to fix it. You may be tempted to dismiss her perception of a problem as imaginary, but that would be a mistake. If one reader stumbles, others may, too, and you would do well to address the issue.

In the extreme circumstance that the normal process of negotiating does not induce your copy editor to undo his editing, you may have to go over his head with a complaint. Please consider this a last resort, after trying first to resolve things with the editor directly. In framing your complaint, try not to assume that the copy editor is stupid or incompetent. If you are being edited by a neophyte, he might not have much practice in breaking rules when it makes sense to do so. Editors at some houses have limited authority to depart from house style. There is always the possibility, too, that you are wrong. In my department, an author once complained to the acquiring editor that the copyediting was capricious and inconsistent. The acquiring editor promised to review the editing with our managing editor—a review that showed that the author had been hasty to judge, probably because of his unfamiliarity with Chicago style. What often happens is that a writer misunderstands some aspect of the editing and loses confidence in the editor. This then colors the writer's response to all the editing. In not bothering to ask the copy editor about her method before complaining, he caused her some temporary humiliation, cost others the time needed to review the editing, and earned a reputation as an alarmist.

Of course, if you're happy with the editing, feel free to say so—to the copy editor herself, to her employers, or in the acknowledgments section of your article or book. Without face-to-face contact, we can't always guess how writers feel. Acknowledgment—or the lack of it—often surprises us. The experience described by a colleague may be typical: as often as not, a writer whose manuscript needed almost no work will praise him effusively, while someone whose book he sweated blood cleaning up will overlook him entirely.

Here's a former colleague's favorite compliment from a writer: "Without changing anything [you] changed everything for the better. Sleight of hand is the editor's best tool." Another colleague was publicly praised in an author's acknowledgments for having the skill "to make her improvements in my text seem like what I was just on the verge of writing myself. But without her, I wouldn't have."

Goodness knows, copy editors aren't in it for the glory—

but when we believe we've brought significant improvement to a project, it can make our day to learn that the writer thinks so, too.

A | As you can see, correct isn't always pretty. So you aren't weird; you're a writer, and one of the things that makes you a writer is that you're sensitive to ugliness. Once you're sensitive to clichés, you'll be all set.

PART TWO

WORKING WITH YOUR
COLLEAGUES AND
WITH YOURSELF

In my experience, most writers are competent and cooperative in their responses to the kinds of problems copy editors grapple with every day. They appreciate our looking at their work and are often apologetic when they see the kinds of housekeeping their copy required.

No, the author is not the enemy. To find the most common causes of our angst and insomnia, we must look closer to home, at difficulties that have nothing to do with the ultimate reception of our work by the writer. In the second half of this book, I will turn to the subject of getting along with ourselves and others on the job. I will write about ways to meet our daily challenges and consider how we sometimes create difficulties for ourselves that we could avoid or remedy by shifting our attitudes and developing new habits.

Some years ago, a study appeared showing that the most stressful work conditions occur when the worker has a great deal of responsibility but very little power. (It's possible that I made that up; nonetheless, it's plausible.) Some of you might think that would include us—after all, we have the responsibilities, the deadlines, the tedium, and the fear that errors will be complained about by authors, noticed by readers, trumpeted by reviewers. And there's the lack of power: we don't set deadlines; we don't set style. In the publishing world, our status is low, our income disproportionate to our education, our skills, and the value we bring to the written project.

If you are reading this book, it is possible that you are just such a stressed-out copy editor. You are an intelligent, sensitive, conscientious soul ready to buckle under the strain of too much work to finish perfectly in too little time. You stay up nights to meet deadlines; you work through weekends. You cry. And that is very wrong; there should be no crying in copyediting.

When you are under pressure to do work that is difficult for any reason, you need some coping strategies. That is what I will try to offer in the remaining chapters.

CHAPTER SEVEN

When Things Get Tough (the Sequel)

THE DANGEROUS MANUSCRIPT

Q | How do you recover from a real proofreading blooper—the kind that has everyone in gales and is terribly embarrassing?

A manuscript can be challenging in many different ways. It can be highly technical or theoretical. It can contain Swahili or Japanese, mathematical equations, complex graphs and tables, inscrutable figures, insider jargon, or hundreds of citations, none of which appear to be consistently styled. It can be badly written; it can be typed with exasperating word-processing techniques. It can just be long.

But to a copy editor, these are all in a day's work. We take the problems line by line, like quilter's stitches, and when we're doing well, we feel competent and in control. We keep track of our decisions on a style sheet; one page at a time, we establish order and coherence where it is lacking.

In my experience, a manuscript becomes "dangerous" in one of two ways. The first is when the tasks it requires seem mindless, that is, overwhelmingly tedious and repetitive; and the second is when the tasks are the opposite of mindless, that is, unusually complicated. In both cases, I worry about taking too much time over them, or doing them badly out of boredom or haste, or introducing errors through careless automation. Faced with dangerous copy, we must do everything we can to prevent the disaster that's waiting to happen.

THE MINDLESS TASK

In a just world, copy editors would never be presented with mindless tasks. It's true that with our sophisticated word-processing tools, we can magically dispense with a great many such chores: numbering, alphabetizing, searching, replacing, formatting. The flip side, however, is that our writers deploy the same tools. Not only does this allow them to create electronic nightmares that we are left to sort out; it also gives them the idea that almost any problem they impose can somehow be handled automatically. But we shouldn't be asked to retype 389 figure numbers and all their corresponding mentions in the text because the author didn't end up getting permission for figure 3. We shouldn't be asked to transpose the first and last names in a fifty-page list of corporate sponsors because the author typed them the wrong way around. We shouldn't be asked to embed footnotes electronically that the author provided in a separate file, or to change the rows in a table to columns.

Nonetheless, we do face such chores, and I have three strategies for tackling them: automate, delegate, or reevaluate.

1. *Automate.* My first strategy for tackling a long, tedious chore is always to find a word-processing shortcut. If the task must be done, and if I believe it can be automated in some way, I will spend two hours trying to figure out how rather than one hour doing it by hand. At least that way I'll know how to do it the next time. I look in a manual, browse online, or as a last re-

sort ask my "guy." (Everyone should have a guy—who of course can be a gal. A guy is someone who knows everything, has endless patience, and is always available and responsive. To maintain good relations with your guy, you must be very careful to bother him only occasionally and only when all else fails. Although I have a fabulous guy, there's a sort of food chain of competence here; I believe that several people actually consider me to be their guy.)

If a task cannot be automated—and assuming that it must be done—I will be blunt about my next strategy: I try to get out of it.

2. *Delegate.* If you are lucky enough to work where the submission guidelines for writers have some bite and the assigning or acquiring editors have some backbone, send the unruly work back "upstairs," as we say at Chicago. It is the author's responsibility to see that his copy conforms to the basic house requirements. They might decide upstairs that an important writer should be let off the hook, but if not, I don't worry about his having to labor over his laptop for a few more hours— that's what hungry interns and grad students are for. If you are lucky enough to work for an office that employs assistants or interns (and if you are ruthless enough to exploit them), another ploy is to toss it their way—although my own rule of thumb is that if my time is too valuable for a particular chore, the same might well be true for an assistant's.

If you are an intern or an assistant or a hungry grad student— well, we thank you. Hang in there; your day will come.

If you are a freelancer, consider asking for help. Your employer or supervising editor might sympathize. She may very well feel that she is paying you to spend your time on more important tasks and agree to find someone else for the more clerical chores. In the boilerplate part of my cover letter to freelancers, I ask them not to take on any time-consuming mechanical task without checking with me first.

Some copy editors employ subcontractors for work that is tedious, specialized, or simply too much to do in the allotted time. This is a legitimate option if it's done with the knowledge of all involved. Your employer is paying you a given rate because she knows your work and values it accordingly. It's not right to turn in the work of someone less experienced and represent it as your own. But if you can define a chunk of the work to be done under your supervision and you accept responsibility for it, your employer might agree.

When you delegate—whether to a freelancer, an assistant, or the author—consider it a privilege, and don't abdicate your fundamental responsibility of oversight. Any time someone else handles electronic files for you, there is the possibility that new errors will end up costing you more trouble than you saved. I rarely let e-files out of my control once I've started working on them. The ideal time to get help is before you start editing, so you can check the corrections as you go. But if there's absolutely nobody waiting in the wings to do your dirty work for you, there is a last resort:

3. *Reevaluate.* If you find that you don't have what it takes to dump a hated task into someone else's lap, consider the possibility that your conscience is trying to tell you something. That is, is it possible that the task should not actually be done by anyone? Sometimes mindless tasks are necessitated by a poorly prepared manuscript, but other times we impose them on ourselves out of a misguided drive to perfect what does not need perfecting.

Any time you find yourself looking at a repetitive task that is going to add a significant amount of time to the editing and that cannot be automated, stop and think about it. Is the offending material actually incorrect, or is it simply not styled conventionally? Will it inconvenience or confuse the reader? Get a second opinion from a colleague. Ask your supervising editor if she thinks it's worth your time. And if finally, after exhausting every effort to make this miserable job go away, you find that it has to be done and it has to be done by you— read on for your bonus strategy.

4. *Accept your fate.* Pitch in and give it your best attention. If it's a truly mechanical task that will take more wrist power than brainpower, put on some background music, treat your-self to coffee or cola (the margarita comes later), and slog away until it's done. Take fun breaks. If it's the sort of thing you can do in small chunks as you edit instead of all at once at the start, that might help prevent those emergency-room visits when the carpal tunnel gives out.

THE COMPLICATED TASK

If a mindless task can cause mental flake-out, a complicated task can cause mental overload. It requires your utmost care and concentration. Let's say an annual report you are edit-ing has been prepared so that the source notes and credits to all the tables and figures are in footnotes that are numbered consecutively with those of the text, instead of having their own numbering system.[1] Not a big deal—since the notes are linked electronically, you simply cut and paste into two sepa-rate hierarchies and all the notes will automatically renumber. A mindless task, but not complicated. However: let's say that throughout both sets of notes, instead of citing each source

1. Some of you will immediately understand and wince; perhaps the rest will take my word that this can cause major headaches.

in full every time (Quentin Dinwiddie, *Zamboni Repair in the Home* [Omaha: Bizboom Press, 2007], appendix 42), the author refers the reader to previous citations by note number ("see n. 198"), and these references are hard-typed, not linked, and must be corrected to match the new numbers. A little trickier. And what if some of the full citations appear in table and figure notes, and others in the notes to the text?

I don't know about you, but when I face tasks like those, I have to fight a fear of getting so entangled in the corrections that I will get off track, not notice until hours later, and then have to undo everything and start over. Let's call this Fear of the Major Undo.

Fear of the Undo may be familiar from other avenues of life. When I was a young mother, I joined a quilting circle. As perfectionists, quilters put copy editors in the shade. If something is the least bit out of whack, they will resolutely rip out hours of stitching and start over. The process is the point, never mind if it takes years to finish. Quilters are so confident of a perfect product that they have a tradition of introducing a flaw into a quilt on purpose, in order not to offend the gods. When I joined this group, I had never been a patient seamstress. (If my mom were around and asked to confirm that, she would probably just crack up laughing.) It was a great goal of mine to develop patience, both in quilting and in life. In time, I actually did achieve a Zenlike patience with a needle.

Unfortunately for me, that level of patience has never extended to any other aspect of life. Nothing puts me in more of a rage than having to revisit work I've already done in order to undo or redo it. Aside from the tedium and waste of time, I suffer knowing that it's nearly impossible to undo an editing decision with the same care and consistency with which I imposed it. I'm doomed to miss a few instances, and that means I will have introduced errors that might not have been there before. I will have done harm. A complicated task, in my view, is one in which the chances are high that you'll do harm. Mindless tasks, with time and patience, can usually be safely undone. The dangerous tasks I'm talking about now are not mindless, and because they involve concentrated decision making to perform, they can involve the same thought and concentration to undo.

This fear of having to undo or redo a complex chore—or even a mindless one—can be a great motivator to consider carefully whether the task is truly necessary in the first place. I would urge you to ask yourself three questions about the current state of the copy before you begin surgery.

1. *Is it wrong?* Often the way a writer organizes/styles/formats his work isn't incorrect; it's just different. If the work follows a respected style guide and it would take a lot of time to rework in your preferred style, follow the four-step strategy I outlined for mindless tasks before you begin (automate, delegate, reevaluate, accept your fate). If it doesn't seem to follow any guide you're familiar with, but it's more or less consistent and makes sense, seriously consider leaving it alone.[2] The last several reference lists I've copyedited were each written in a unique hybrid of recognized styles. One author put all dates in parentheses; one put "ed." in parentheses; one reversed all author names in multiauthor works (Boyer, S. G.). All were nicely prepared, internally consistent, and unambiguous. I made whatever changes I could automate and left the rest.

---

2. Not all editors have the option to ignore house style. The styling of source citations for most journals, for instance, is nonnegotiable. Fortunately, most journals also have fairly strict standards that writers must adhere to when submitting their work, so returning a substandard manuscript to the writer for another pass might be feasible.

2. Is it confusing? "Confusing" is a lesser form of "wrong" and calls for intervention. When all the legends to a series of pie charts list the percentages in alphabetical order instead of in order of quantity, it's not wrong—but it makes it harder for the reader to see at a glance who gets the biggest piece of the pie. When an author uses bibliography style for citations in the notes, inverting first name and last, putting periods or commas instead of semicolons between the elements, and so forth, a reader can barely tell where one citation begins and another ends:

> 32. Lynne, N. 1994. "The Chicken or the Egg?" In *Hysteron Proteron.* Ed. M. Parish. Cambridge, pp. 32–117, Dawn, R. 1958. "Spacing and Spacing Out: Unreasonable Reasonings." *Miseologus* 3:244–49.

These kinds of blemishes have to be fixed. But sometimes an unconventional method works just fine. In a one-of-a-kind bibliography with consistent styling, does it really matter where the date appears, or whether chapter titles are in quotation marks? If the legend to a pie chart is short, simple, and color-matched to the pie, mightn't it work in alphabetical order? If you had all the time in the world to spend micro-tinkering such kinks into conformity with your rules, that would be great—but you don't. And while you're busy pouncing on every little dust bunny, you may be overlooking the monster under the bed—that is, more important problems with the content. Bottom line: if an odd style has logic and clarity, and if your institution gives you any measure of flexibility in the matter, leave well enough alone.

When I said as much in a reply to a query to the "Chicago Style Q&A," the writer wrote back with some impatience:

Hmm, yes, and thank you for your reply. Is the following a fair summary of your message?

· Stop wasting time.
· Adhere to the style manual, except when you don't feel like it.

He pretty much nailed it—if we refine "when you don't feel like it" to "when it's not working."

3. Is it ugly? There is the occasional instance in which a writer's decision isn't wrong or confusing, but, aesthetically speaking, you know it will lie badly on the page. For instance, a surfeit of numbers in running text can be an eyesore and tiresome to readers. The information might be better cast as a chart or table. On the other hand, material worked into tables is itself prone to ugliness: creating a table is far more difficult than criticizing or reshaping one that's already been made, and the creator of the table is often too close to the data to perceive the reader's problem with it. A long, skinny table might look better broken into two columns, for instance. Or sometimes a table's side and top headings ought to be flipped to allow more room for longer headings. People might naturally disagree about such matters if they ultimately depend more on personal taste than expertise, but the point remains that a copy editor should consider modifying features that will put the reader off, even if it calls for a bit of extra effort.

Once you've considered a complex editing issue and decided it must be done, lean on two of the virtues we talked about in part 1: carefulness and transparency. The first helps prevent mistakes; the second will help you check your work and undo it if you get into a fix. I narrowly escaped trouble when I meddled with the initial capping of Shakespeare quotations in a book about the Bard. I started out tracking my changes "like this" and "Like this" for the writer's benefit. But after I had marked enough to give the writer the idea of my method, I continued silently. If the writer had wanted his original system reinstated (luckily, he opted for Chicago's style), I would have had to comb through the original document, carefully searching for the altered quotations (among many non-Shakespeare quotations that followed style), to find the errors. The transparency of redlining would have helped, but asking first (another kind of transparency) would have been better.

A third use of transparency is to send the writer a sample of the reworked material in order to show her what you're doing before it's too late to change your mind.

WHEN WE GOOF

A terrible truth is that copy editors make mistakes. And as a copy editor, I can tell you that when mistakes happen, it's not easy for us. We are the correctors. We don't handle it well when we mess up. We're better at denying and rationalizing and finger-pointing.

But are we not human? Why shouldn't we err? One study on human error rates concludes that "the best performance possible in well managed workplaces using normal quality management methods [has] failure rates of 5 to 10 in every hundred opportunities."[3]

Nevertheless, in some pursuits, there's an idea that perfection can be attained. When surgeons mess up, or airline pilots, or dry cleaners, or wedding planners, expect lawsuits.

3. David J. Smith, *Reliability, Maintainability and Risk*, 7th ed. (Oxford: Elsevier, 2005), app. 6, http://dx.doi.org/10.1016/B978 -075066694-7/50031-4.

Even in creative fields, where the real-life stakes are arguably lower than in surgery, we believe in perfection. Remember the quilters? And poets—don't get me started.

Difficult documents increase the odds of catastrophe. And when we make mistakes, there's no point in hoping that no one will notice. The only time I was able to make a mess of a manuscript without annoying the author was the time a severely dyslexic writer reviewed the editing and page proofs himself. Did I get away with murder? Not a chance. To my humiliation I read in a published review, "Finally, I must mention that this volume is poorly edited for a product from a major university press. Typographical errors and redundancies abound." At the time, I had many excuses and explanations for how, in spite of what I considered extraordinary efforts on my part to perfect that nightmare copy, more than the usual number of errors slipped into print. But there was no escaping the fact that it had been my responsibility. My biggest mistake was in not advising the publisher to hire a professional proofreader at the page-proof stage, knowing as I did that we wouldn't read it in-house and the author wasn't up to the task.

In that case, there was nothing I could do to put things right, but usually a major editing goof will be discovered when the writer or your supervisor reviews the editing, and you will have to fix it. Consider this part of the job and give it your best attention. Make apologies. Let the author see the cleaned-up version if there's time and your supervising editor agrees. In a book project, if the author is reviewing page proofs, that might be the best time for him to check that everything has been corrected.

Sometimes you will come to regret an editing decision in the middle of the job, before the writer ever has a chance to see it. If it's something that occurs frequently in the work, something you can't easily fix by going back and searching, you're in trouble. Let's say that in a work where *He* and *Him* are upper-cased when referring to God, you decide to lowercase them, per house style. The writer doesn't seem to be expressing a theological point of view; the caps are out of place and mis-leading; lowercasing is your style; and—the clincher—the caps aren't consistently imposed. Then, later on, the capped pronouns proliferate. There are dozens and dozens of them, and every last one of them is capped. The author explains in a footnote that he caps them because his mother asked him to. On her deathbed.

Searching for lowercased pronouns like *he* and *him* is go-ing to take a while, but just be glad you have a chance to do it now.

Before you begin any time-consuming task, you should of course seriously ponder whether it really matters. Sometimes you might conclude that an issue doesn't deserve the time you would have to devote to sorting it out. Say you run into a sentence where the writer starts out using the pronoun *one* ("One might think that this is true") but switches to *you* part-way ("in spite of everything you learned in kindergarten"), so you change *one* to *you*. On the next page you find another *one*, and even though it's just fine there on its own, since you changed the last *one* to *you*, you change this *one* as well. Pretty soon you're on a misguided mission to rid the copy of *ones*—until you get distracted by something else. A few dozen pages later, you remember and start worrying that you let a few get by you. Aargh. Is it worth your time to reread for just this is-sue? (No.) Will the author notice? (Probably, since your previ-ous hen tracks will give you away.)

A good strategy in such a case is to mention the matter when you hand over the work for review. That way, if the author cares enough, he can keep an eye out for it as he reads. To help prevent his dismay, point out why the styling is optional or the issue not that important. ("Early on, I paid attention to your use of *you* vs. *one*, but at some point the issue seemed to lose importance, probably because there's really nothing wrong with the variation, other than within a given sentence. If you care to put back anything I changed in this regard or make further changes for the sake of consistency, please feel free.") Don't make a big deal out of small matters—if it were a big deal, you would have gone back and fixed it. ("I think it's sometimes good to repeat the poem number when you resume discussion of a poem after a digression. I wasn't rigid about it; I added them whenever I found myself thinking 'wait—which poem are we in?' Add more if you like, or strike mine if you think they're intrusive.")

Sometimes, no matter how hard you try, you aren't going to be able to rationalize away an editing error that ends up in the hands of the author. Not long ago I edited a novel—a rarity for me—in which the main character professed to be a famous (historically real) Spanish explorer from the past. Although the character's name was properly accented on the title page, the accent was inconsistently applied throughout the rest of the book. I wasn't surprised—many writers omit accents when they type, either overlooking them or slothfully assuming they'll be put in by someone later. So right away I zapped them all into place, hundreds of them, with a lightning search-and-replace. I didn't give it another thought until I received the editing back from the author with a kindly explanation of why it was important to remove the accents I had added. Remember—this was fiction. It turned out that the author hadn't overlooked a thing and had not a slothful bone in his body, but in his meticulous and ingenious way, he had omitted the accent *only* in any use of the name by a present-day American character. We debated whether this distinction would be lost on readers, but like much good fiction, this novel was built upon many such subtleties, the sum of which provided a delightful complexity.[4] I had goofed; the issue was important to the writer; I had no choice but to take the time to remove the accents, one by one.

. . .

So far in this chapter, if I have skirted the further dangers that can arise when we try to automate complex tasks, it's not because I take it for granted that each of you has mastered your word processor. Rather, it's because I think word-processing issues deserve a chapter all their own. Read on.

> **A** | Naturally, we have very little experience with this. Is there absolutely no way to blame it on someone else? If not, you probably should keep a low profile until it blows over. Lucky for you, proofreaders automatically have a fairly low profile.

---

4. Delightful to the reader who notices it, that is. A copy editor would rather have a spoiler in the form of a heads-up from the writer.

CHAPTER EIGHT

Know Thy Word Processor

Q / What do you say (or do) to an author who makes extensive revisions (without tracking) to his original manuscript after you have sent him the copyedited version? Just wondering . . .

If, in copyediting, a little learning is a dangerous thing, the same is doubly so in word processing, where lightning can strike with one peck of your pinkie. While you are making it your business to master your chosen style rules, you must make a similar priority of mastering your word-processing application. Although word-processing software is capable of automating many vexing tasks, it is also capable of making the most exquisite mess of your work.

As a supervisor of twenty-somethings, I was surprised to realize that college students—even computer-savvy techie types—are not necessarily competent at word processing. They know how to type a paper, possibly insert some footnotes or endnotes, and add page numbers. They know how to jazz up a document with funky fonts and colors. They might have played around enough to discover the prefab heading styles and margin settings. They definitely know where to find the spell-checker.

As a copy editor, you must know far, far more to do your job efficiently. I will go further: if you charge money for editing services and you aren't an expert word processor, you're not doing honest work. Worse, you can't possibly enjoy your work if you are constantly stressed over miserable computer issues. Becoming competent and perhaps even expert at the keyboard has untold benefits: you'll be faster, more accurate, more confident, more valuable ($$!)—are you sold yet on this idea?

Entire books and classes are devoted to the how-tos of word processing, so that is not my purpose here. Because readers of this book use a variety of applications, and because software capabilities change so rapidly, I will focus more generally on the pitfalls of editing on-screen and how we can cope with them.

ME? A TECHIE?

In my line of work, I hear a lot about the annoyances of working on a computer. People hate it when their word processor springs a pop-up in the middle of certain tasks, or vetoes perfectly good grammar, or automatically uses the Calibri font, or capitalizes words meant to be lowercased, or selects a whole word when they want to select only part of it.

What many writers and editors don't seem to understand is that computers do as they're told and would be happy (so to speak) to do your bidding. We can tell them what to do! Although detailed customizing takes a bit of time and trouble, there is a quick and easy shortcut to disciplining the features you use most. Find the Options section of your word-processing program. This is where it begs, "Just tell me what you want." Clicking around, you'll find dozens of checkboxes.

Reviewing all the choices takes only a few minutes. With one click, you can make the grammar-checker stop forever—unless you invite it back in later, of course. You can choose which toolbars are visible and even which icons are visible on each toolbar. Me? I would rather superglue my fingers to the keyboard than have squiggly lines under allegedly misspelled words.[1] Click—they're gone.

If there's something in particular you want to adjust, and assuming you work in a widely used application, you don't need to spend hours mousing around in the Options in order to find it. Just type (e.g.) "MS Word cursor settings" or "adding comments to PDF" into Google or Bing, and all will be revealed.

Learning to use keyboard shortcuts instead of motoring around the screen with a mouse is an excellent way to start improving your skills, because shortcuts are fun and easy and can save you time and physical pain from mouse-steering. Many shortcuts are already built into your application, and you can assign your own as well. With shortcuts you can navigate quickly within and between documents, choose items from menus, apply and remove formatting, cut and paste text, expand and collapse windows—really almost anything you like—all by tapping a couple of keys and involving no contact with rodents.

To inspire you, let me list a few tasks that can be accomplished in literally a few seconds when you know how:

- alphabetizing long lists
- title casing text that's in all caps

1. No, I'm not so confident of my spelling prowess that I don't use the spell-checker. But I do it as one of the last steps of editing. I like to see what I missed.

- restyling all the footnote (or endnote) numbers in a book at once
- changing the columns in a table into rows and vice versa
- doing multiple cleanup tasks at once with a single one-click macro

When you venture past the basics of word processing, the amount of information will be overwhelming, so make a short list of the operations that you most want to learn. You can start small: post the key commands for one or two new tricks on a sticky near your monitor. When those become second nature, move on.

There are excellent sites online that give word-processing tips and tricks. The Editorium offers downloadable macros that make quick work of tasks like cleaning up tabs and spacing, unembedding notes, and turning automatic bullets or numbers into real ones.[2] Experiment with recording your own macros for chores you repeat often.[3]

Finally, don't forget human resources: the advantage of asking a fellow copy editor when you're stuck is that, unlike your computer, he knows your job and will understand exactly what you are trying to do—and what you don't want to happen. You may also subscribe to an e-mailing list of editors who will respond to a posted query. When you post a question, consider waiting for more than one response. Sometimes an added caveat will save you from bad advice.

2. Go to http://www.editorium.com/. There are many free resources here: Editorium's "Advanced Find and Replace for Microsoft Word" looks complicated on first reading, but if you have already figured out how to do wildcard searches in Word, going to this next level is not really so difficult, and learning it could add years to your life.
3. If macros intrigue you, take a look at a baby-steps intro on my blog: http://www.subversivecopyeditor.com/blog/2012/08/lets-make-a-macro.html.

COLLISION INSURANCE: FIVE WAYS TO AVOID MAJOR DAMAGE

Learning techniques to speed up your work through computer shortcuts can be intoxicating, but remember: you're the designated driver here. Who among us has never in haste saved the wrong version over the right one, or recognized too late an ill-conceived global search-and-replace? I have personal knowledge of a work that contained references to the Paris Peach Conference, and another whose author caught in the nick of time several mentions of trouble with the Genitals in his work on Jewish-Gentile relations. And then there was the astrophysics text where two fluid elements in "causal contact" came to be in "casual contact" (which, I now know, is not at all the same thing). If you've escaped trouble this far, maybe it's because you know five important practices of e-file management.

1. *Labels and folders.* Although it's possible to get through life with all your documents in one vast folder in your file manager, why would anyone do that, when it's so easy to create discrete folders, and folders within folders? (I could go on, but then you'd think I'm neurotic about folders.) Seriously, some jobs require more filing than others. If your work is project-oriented, it makes sense to have a folder for each project. If your work is more scattershot and ephemeral, you might do better to stay on top of clearing files into Stuff to Delete Someday and Stuff to Hang On To. The point is to give thought to how you're going to find what you need, either now or later. If you have a supervisor or colleagues who need access to your work, this is even more important. To get organized, consider (a) how long you'll need the materials, (b) who needs access, (c) whether you need to identify different versions, archive subsequent versions, or lock the original versions. And (d),

if thinking about creating folders makes you twitch, you absolutely must take care when naming your files. Computer search functions are already excellent and can only improve, but they can only do so much if you have a hundred files labeled "Contract." With all that in mind, set up a system and spend a few minutes a day keeping it in order.

Filing is a personal issue. I can't tell you that one way is better than another. But it's not hard to see how tossing documents any old place and letting them pile up can lead to embarrassment, panic, duplication of work already done, and a general feeling of hopeless incompetence. So try to summon some self-discipline in this area. I admit that I was once somewhat enslaved to my filing system, and at some point it probably does become counterproductive to nest the folders too deeply, so create your filing hierarchy in a way that works best for you, and if you find it's getting out of hand, well, maybe there's a twelve-step program for you.

2. *Trial runs.* Word-processing programs do everything they can to prevent you from losing your work. They let you undo even after saving, and they automatically save your work even when you crash. Even so, when you're about to try something complex and experimental while editing, there's good reason not to gamble with your working document. Save a copy under a new name, like Test 1, and see how it works out before you inflict it for keeps. Here's why: you might not notice a problem caused by your tricky moves until after you've done further editing and closed the application. At that point, it's great to have a choice between undoing the mess and starting over.

One danger I've run into with test files: I get up to find coffee, stop to chat with Joe in Production, text my kids before I get back to the monitor—and forget that the file open on the screen is not my working document. I once worked for an hour editing the wrong version. Another time, I didn't label the test file clearly and accidentally saved it over the correct version when I was in a hurry to finish. I wanted to kill somebody. To prevent confusion now, I like to color the font in my test file. I find olive green to be soothing.

3. *Version control.* If you frequently consult original files while working in subsequent versions, clearly labeled documents can help you avoid confusion. It's also a good idea to lock any files you need to preserve, in addition to saving them on a backup drive.

If you are sending electronic files to a writer for vetting, it's essential to keep straight who has the working copy. If the author is busy making changes and corrections at the same time you're adding final tweaks, even if both of you are scrupulous about tracking every change, you will have confusion. Depending on the nature of the author's tasks, you might decide to lock the files so the author cannot turn off tracking.

4. *Sharing.* An added point of going to so much trouble with labels and versions is that occasionally someone other than you might have to find something in your computer. More likely, someone else will handle your files when they're in final form and it's time to send them to the client or for typesetting. Labels that are clear to everyone rather than in your own secret code are essential at that point.

5. *Backup.* My son Ben used to work in computer tech support and heard quite a few war stories from the veterans. He told me that one of the first things he learned was how to handle the arrogance and rage of crash victims, often directed at the technician. He was advised to reassure the person, and if he could get the computer up and running, he should say, "Okay, great—now if you'll just give me your backup files,

we'll put everything back the way it was." Then, inevitably, came the victim's deer-in-the-headlights face as she realized whose fault it was that there was no backup.

Backing up computer files is so easy—why do so many people not do it? Many of us have lost work that wasn't backed up: We save an old version over the new one; our laptop is stolen along with the backup thumb drive plugged into it; we forget to save in the first place, and just when we're getting ready to, one of the kids—the one who plays bass in a rock band—plugs his amplifier into the electric circuit that includes the clothes dryer and the basement office computer. (Not that any of that has happened to me.)

OK, so I was a loser. But my losses are your gain, because the pain of losing my work and having to redo it is something I've had time to ponder more than once, and because of that I've given some thought to preventing it. Backing up isn't what it used to be. These days, when you can back up work online automatically at minimal or no cost, there's just no excuse for not doing it.[4]

First, though, it helps to be clear on one's personal backup philosophy. In the old days, I thought that backing up needed to include every datum generated by my computer. I accumulated stacks of CDs, then a series of thumb drives. These days I feel fine backing up only my active projects. Weirdly, the experience of losing everything can be therapeutic. I've learned that after a while old files become so much baggage. Starting over can be liberating. You probably don't really need it all. In any case, identifying your archives and separating them from work you want to back up regularly can save you time and space and money.

4. I'm talking about backing up the personal computer files of a regular joe professional. If your work involves megatons of research data, you probably already back up to institutional or paid servers.

Almost no time or space or money is needed to use an online service like Dropbox or IDrive that allows you to access your files from any computer that you install their free software on, or from any other computer by logging in at the service's website. Updates to documents sync automatically, and you can share files easily with others, either by posting them in a public folder or by e-mailing someone a link to a private folder. If you aren't online when you work on a document, changes will be synced whenever you're next online. Security involves extra-super-duper encryption-whatever, which I confess I take on blind faith—whatever it is, it's surely more secure than a thumb drive hanging out of a USB port. And you can pay for more space or enhanced services.

I know there's no need to belabor the point. Back up as much as you need in order not to want to slit your wrists if you lose the rest.

RESISTING COMPULSION

There are many obvious reasons why computer editing is superior to editing on paper. It allows us to add and delete copy cleanly, to make our editing visible or invisible as we choose, to take care of repetitive tasks efficiently and consistently. We can e-mail documents to others both in-house and out, and the finished document can go to typesetting with the expectation of fewer typos in page proofs than otherwise. Although in the early days of electronic word processing most of us probably believed it would save time and paper (and therefore money), I doubt that many of us find that to be true. We print because we can—I see no evidence of a green movement in my office. And as for saving time? My editing schedules have not changed significantly in twenty-five years. The time we save in automating tasks, we lose in having to prepare the files for typesetting.[5] What we save in not hand marking, we lose in a hundred other little tasks that we do because it's so easy we can't resist.

And that is the challenge: to rein in our compulsive tendencies in favor of efficiency. Just because we can doesn't mean we should. It bears repeating: if you are about to embark on a time-consuming task, remember your three-step emergency mantra: automate, delegate, reevaluate. It's possible to accumulate hours of wasted time out of compulsion and ignorance. One editor I know didn't like the way Word uses superscripted note numbers in the notes pane instead of placing them full-sized on the line with a period, so one by one, for each of hundreds of notes, she highlighted the number, formatted it to Not Superscript (using her mouse and the menu), and typed a period after it—a chore that she could have accomplished for the entire document in less than twenty seconds using keyboard commands.[6]

We'll return to the topic of our compulsions later. For now, let's continue thinking about efficiency and the reasons we need to stop wasting time. In the next chapter, let's think about deadlines.

A | Please use your imagination; we would rather not say. (As for the manuscript, Microsoft Word's "Compare" feature might help.)

---

5. A common complaint among copy editors is that our responsibilities have been extended to include a great deal of preproduction work that we are not trained for and have little interest in. The formula in my department is to add an extra 20 percent to the estimate of editing hours for cleaning up the original files (stripping out formatting, odd spacing, stray tabs, etc.), assigning typesetting codes, and updating the files after the writer has reviewed the editing.

6. Okay—I will admit that this was me. But it was a long time ago, and I recognized that I had a problem and sought help.

CHAPTER NINE

The Living Deadline

Q | Is it "cell phone" or "cel phone"? I am working on a crash deadline, and would appreciate a quick response. Thank you so much!

The writer Douglas Adams famously claimed to love deadlines: "I love deadlines," he said. "I like the whooshing sound they make as they fly by."

Isn't that adorable.

We love writers, and we indulge them for their quirky, creative genius. But the rest of us have to meet our deadlines, and the letters to the "Chicago Style Q&A" attest to that in force. Some schedules are more firm than others—obviously, the timing of newspapers and magazines allows little wiggle room. Although most book deadlines have at least some room to slide—and many do, by days, weeks, or even years—that is never the goal, and a copy editor who consistently misses deadlines will mark herself as unreliable.

Some delays in publishing are outside the copy editor's control, even when the copy is in her own hands. The electronic files may be corrupted. Parts of the document might be missing. A writer sends late-breaking information that must be added. Even after the editing is finished, when the editor is preparing the copy for production, the design specifications might be late, or permissions to use material incomplete, or an illustration found to be substandard. The writer may be unreachable. (One editor told me about a delay over some missing sources that the writer couldn't send because his wife was holding his research hostage in the end stages of their divorce.) Sometimes a minor delay compounds as it precipitates another: say a photographer who agreed to a photo shoot by a certain date is stalled by your publicity department's failure to send the right props; the photographer is booked with other projects, thereby turning a week's delay into a month's delay.

Hang-ups outside your control are just that; all you can do is make your team or your supervisor aware of them. Given the short schedules at newspapers and magazines, delays can deep-six a project altogether. If your writer is directly responsible for a delay, your prompts and gentle naggings might be the only thing saving it from being scrapped. It can be especially tempting for editors of book manuscripts to shrug at deadlines when it begins to seem as though a project has little chance of delivery at the targeted date no matter how watchful you are. But that attitude is damaging both to the publishing team and to yourself. The economic damage is predictable: seasonal lists and budgets are planned to accommodate average delays. If everyone slacks off because "delays don't matter," the average delay will grow, and that's not good for the financial health of your company. In more personal terms, inattention to deadlines will inconvenience everyone who follows you in the assembly line. You will become . . . unpopular.

To manage your deadlines, become proficient in three skills: prioritizing, organizing, and documentizing.[1]

PRIORITIZING: FOUR QUESTIONS TO HELP YOU PLAN

Copy editors have a million things to do. Either we handle several overlapping projects or we handle multiple tasks within a single project. If we aren't freelancers ourselves, we supervise freelancers. My to-do list on a typical day as a manuscript editor might include e-mailing a PDF of page proofs to an author, editing an index, putting a finished project into production, cleaning up a manuscript that's come back from an author, making notes on a new project for an editorial meeting, checking permission letters against an author's figure credits—never mind actually reading the book I'm in the middle of editing. Your list will be similarly full.

You can't do all those things in one day, even if they're due. But you do have some choices: you can freak out and take a sick day; you can stay up all night drinking coffee; or you can figure out which chores are most urgent, get them done by five, then call up a beau and go dancing. You pick.

Triaging your projects can be agonizing unless you develop some guidelines. Here are four questions to weigh when you can't decide what to do first.

1. *Is it next?* A good rule of thumb is that, all else being equal, the project that's nearest to production or publication

---

1. If you aren't reading this, it's because *documentizing* didn't make it past the copy editor. [Note to copy editor: *Oxford English Dictionary*, 2nd ed.: "documentize, *v. trans.* **a.** To teach, instruct, give a lesson to. **b.** To furnish with evidence." Yes, it's obsolete, but I wanted a word with *zing!*]

gets the attention. That is, if the agenda for tomorrow's board of directors' meeting lands on your desk just when you were getting ready to tackle next quarter's newsletter to investors, the agenda wins. If the Kimball index lands in your tray when you were getting ready to look at the Hannigan manuscript just back from the author, the index trumps the manuscript for your attention, because indexing is one of the last stages of production. When typesetting is involved, it's more likely that end-stage delays will inconvenience others. By that time, folks in production and publicity will have assumed much of the responsibility for getting the title delivered and promoted on time, and they're probably juggling twice as many projects as you. If you hold things up, you're likely to interfere with their typesetting and promotion schedules. At the start of a project, however, it's all yours.

2. *Is it most important?* For whatever reason, some projects are more important than others, either because they're big moneymakers or because the client or writer is a heavyweight. When you bump one task for another for the reason of importance, remember that it's not necessary to explain in detail to a writer or client the reasons work isn't progressing as planned. After all, what can you say? "I'm so sorry about the delay— I was attending to a more important project"? Unless it's your boss who's asking, just apologize for the delay; don't explain: "I'm sorry this is taking longer than expected; if all goes well, I should be able to send you everything by the end of the week. I'll keep you posted."

3. *Is it most urgent?* Magazine and journal articles with rigid delivery dates can't wait. Corporations have legal imperatives to publish certain reports at set times of the fiscal year. Books can also have important delivery dates, planned for optimal marketing around a holiday, annual conference, or textbook

season. Or a piece might be rushed because it treats a political or popular issue that's hot this minute but doomed to fade. (Remember that scandal at the Reykjavík Salmon Summit of 1988? Me neither.)

Short, urgent tasks should get your immediate attention. A task can also be urgent if holding it up will cause a consequent additional delay; for instance, if you don't get the edited copy to a writer by Friday, he'll be unable to look at it for two weeks. Once, I had two urgent tasks and decided which one would have to wait, not realizing that the designer who would handle it after me was leaving on vacation the next day. Too late, I wished I'd e-mailed her to say, "I'm not sure I can get the Willard revises to you today—is tomorrow just as good?"

4. *Is it the right thing to do?* Sometimes a task might not be the most urgent or important, but you promised it in such a way that your conscience won't let you shove it aside. Those are tough choices, but you'll sleep better if you honor your promise. You know what I mean: one of those desperately caring authors who sweats blood over every decision e-mails you to ask whether it might be better to convert tables 2, 6, 32, and 34 into text, and you promise to look at them as soon as possible, and you know he's wringing his hands until it's decided. If you're displacing an important or urgent task, you might have to put in some overtime until you're caught up.

Some caveats: First, don't make a habit of promising anything, especially in response to demanding personalities— just tell Maynard in Design that you'll get to his pet task as soon as you can, and be specific about when, if possible. And second, when you communicate an expected delay, it's better to tell than ask. If you ask ("Do you mind if that's a few days late?"), you might not get the answer you're hoping for. Unless you're fishing for information that will help you order your tasks, it's better to simply say or write, "The Herrmann piece is going to be a few days late. I'm aiming to get it to you on Tuesday next week." If it turns out that your delay will cause a major problem, you'll no doubt hear about it, and you can always reconsider.

Finally, be aware of the way you work best, and take that into account when faced with competing tasks from various projects. If you get confused flipping back and forth between the works of different writers (because it involves switching your brain between two very different styles—or worse, only slightly different styles), try not to do that. Instead, give the Oaks proposal your full attention until you've done all you can with it.

ORGANIZING

This section is a tough one, but I'd really like you to read it. Think of this as the vegetable section. If you work in publishing, being organized is good for your health. If you're already a well-organized editor, take a vitamin and skip this part. If you're a veggie lover, all the better.

An old Chinese proverb that happens to feature a vegetable (well, technically a fruit, but I don't want this to be the fruit section) says, "One cannot manage too many affairs: like pumpkins in the water, one pops up while you try to hold down the other." The trouble is, we've got the pumpkins. The question is, how to keep track of them.

Organization is a personal matter. Some like nothing better than to poke at pumpkins, and others would rather just hang on to one at a time. As you know by now, I tend to be a hyper-

filing, to-do-list type of gal, but I have known other systems to
work. Everyone knows someone who organizes by the "stack"
method. During the years I worked acquiring children's books,
one colleague was famous for this. No one could imagine how
she found anything in the piles of paper on her desk, on the
credenza, on the filing cabinet, and on the floor. Yet I never
knew her to lose anything, and she was more prompt than
anyone in returning manuscripts I wanted her opinion on. She
said she returned things quickly so she wouldn't lose them—
her own style of efficiency.

That said, there are a few organizing tools that are indis-
pensable to any professional. *Lists* give you a picture of the
short term, *schedules* show the longer-term view, and *logs* keep
track of what you've already done. All three are worth a closer
look. Let's make a list.

1. *Lists.* A simple to-do list is an excellent aid. Think of it as
the editor's broccoli. I keep an e-list on my computer desktop
and click it open first thing every morning and keep it open
all day. Whenever I need to remind myself to do something, I
type it in, more or less in order of urgency. I can delete tasks
when they're done or rearrange their order. My other, personal,
nonwork to-do list is in an app on my phone.

Young readers, stop rolling your eyes! ("Like, who could
forget this stuff?") Those pushing middle age or older will be
nodding in recognition of my wisdom. I tend to make reminders for meetings, tasks, and pre-deadline deadlines, but a list
can be as detailed as you like and in whatever form suits you.
My office has online schedules and calendars, but those don't
reflect my own plans for the day. Many of my colleagues write
tasks and meetings on desk-blotter calendars; others paste
yellow stickies around their monitors and bookshelves. One
has even mentioned leaving voice-mail reminders for herself.

Whatever works. The advantage of my little written list is that one glance at the top of it tells me what to do next.

2. *Schedules.* Think spinach. Here at the U of C Press, we have an amazing online schedule that allows each of us to see our project deadlines in any number of displays tailored to the information we request. My favorite is a list of the tasks I'm responsible for in the next two weeks. I open it each morning to get a look at what's on the horizon. In contrast to my to-do list, which prioritizes tasks for today, the schedule includes looming deadlines for projects that are out of my hands at the moment, prompting me to check in with authors and colleagues concerning their progress. If the schedule shows that an edited manuscript is due back from the writer in a week, I might shoot a quick e-mail in that direction. ("Just checking in. Have you had a chance to look at the editing? Do you expect to have it back to me next week?") If a manuscript is slated for typesetting soon and I don't have everything I need, that's a prompt to send reminders. ("Dorman is ready to go as soon as I have design specs. Just wanted to let you know.")

If you don't have a high-tech schedule to consult, creating even a rudimentary one will help you meet your deadlines. A list on paper, an online calendar, or an e-file like my to-do list—all are handy guides to what's happening when.

3. *Logs.* Totally organic. I'm going to mention logs here because they are good organizing tools, even though they tend to focus on what's finished, rather than what's not, and in that way they aren't especially relevant to deadline control. Administrators keep logs out of necessity—part of their job is to account for how much work was done and how long it took and how much it cost. Freelancers need logs, probably best kept in the form of spreadsheets, to keep track of clients, fees, and income from each job. Software can sort the information into various displays: jobs done for a particular client, total income

from one type of editorial service, or whatever is needed—all very handy at tax time. Project managers, likewise, can keep a spreadsheet log of freelancers, with dates in and out, rates per hour or page, invoice totals, contact information, and anything else that is useful.

My log is a personal tool and very simple. At the end of each day, I type what I did. Here's one day (if my log doesn't make sense to you, yours will): "Feb. 20. Gilfoyle ed. notes. C&P final lasers. Edit Brown, to 216. Mtg. w/ JT, SMH, & PDK re Baker schedule."

I was inspired to start my log years ago when I seemed to be in a malaise: at the end of one day, I was ashamed at how little I'd done—well, we all have those days. But I knew it hadn't been just that day, and I resolved to start accounting to myself for my time. What began as a motivational tool, however, evolved into more as I found myself referring to it for information that had expired from my schedules and to-do lists. I often consult the log when I need to recall a project that has been on the back burner for a while before contacting an author or nudging a coworker.

Altogether, lists, schedules, and logs take only a minute or two each day to update and are among the best possible uses of your time, considering the amount of time and confusion they can save. Plus, I promise they will give you whiter teeth and stronger bones.

DOCUMENTIZING[2]

Even when all your pumpkins are under control, they're only yours temporarily, and at some point you'll be handing them

2. By now I feel committed to the word.

off. Keeping others apprised of fluctuations in your schedules is an important part of managing deadlines. It's no help for you to finish early if the stage isn't set for the next act. And if you're running late, the person waiting on you wants to know it sooner rather than later. If you're part of a publishing team, you need to know what's promised to whom, and when. And because such things can change unpredictably, you need to keep track of everyone's latest requests, promises, and updates so you can refer to them regularly.

E-mail has become the most common and efficient way to keep records of this sort. Phone calls are sometimes necessary—even preferable, for the personal touch—and certainly you can make notes of a conversation as you talk, but e-mail takes up less space and can be speedily searched. For this reason, I see e-mail management as the best tool for documenting deadline-related information.

Whole books have been published on the subject of managing e-mail, but for the copy editor, the basics can be boiled down to three: (1) order, (2) discipline, and (3) etiquette. The first two are relevant here; I'll talk about etiquette in the next chapter.

1. *E-mail order.* I used to frown on yards-long unsorted in-boxes, but search functions in e-mail platforms have become so efficient that as long as you have space in your in-box, filing messages in folders might reasonably be optional for you. That said, if you often need to locate important messages, take whatever steps you need to make them findable. How many times have you stood waiting for information while someone scrolled and clicked and scrolled and clicked, muttering, "I know it's here somewhere"? If your work is project-based, a folder for each project allows you to click through a sequence of correspondence efficiently; it also makes it easy to archive

all the related messages when the project expires. Locating information is only one problem. Another is that unless you are scrupulous about reading and responding to every message before it gets bumped off the bottom of the in-box screen, soon there will be a number of messages that are out of sight—and out of mind. Invisible and unanswered. Which leads to the next point.

2. *E-mail discipline.* Whether you read your incoming messages the minute they arrive or once an hour or once a day, staying on top of them is imperative if you want to maintain good work relationships and keep abreast of news that affects your deadlines. I find it appalling when my second query about something is met with "I'm sorry—I must have missed your first message somehow." It's one of those rare areas of work etiquette that I believe to be nonnegotiable: when a client or employer sends you a work-related message, you respond, immediately if possible. The temptation is strong to delay answering until you can write at length, until you can look something up, until you can report that the task is finished—but of course by then the message has fallen off your screen and out of your brain. And don't tell me you don't have time. In five seconds or less, you can hit Reply, type "Thanks" or "Done" or "I'm on it" or "Will do," and hit Send. "More to come!" and "Stay tuned . . ." take a couple of seconds at most. If you aren't on such breezy terms with your correspondent, it's not hard to add a bit of formality: "Nan, I'm sorry I'm in a rush at the moment, but I'll get back to you ASAP. Best, Carol."

Work relationships with colleagues are different from those with clients and bosses in that some of them evolve to the point where you understand each other without response, in which case e-mail chatter becomes a nuisance. But coworkers outside your inner circle deserve the respect of a prompt reply.

A system that works well for me is to use my in-box only for messages I haven't finished with. In effect, it's another to-do list. Everything else gets trashed or filed immediately. If you decide to use folders, don't forget to sort the out-box. The odds that my out-box at work would contain an unsorted e-mail if you were to leap from behind my cubicle wall and check it are almost nil. I'm sorry if I'm beginning to sound superior, but I can't help it. At work, I am the queen of e-mail discipline. In my personal e-mail account, however, I don't bother.

A | Anyone who has deadlines should also have a dictionary. I always swear I'm not going to look up words for people, but it's like being a mom and picking up socks—something just makes me do it. It's "cell phone." Please buy a dictionary—and pick up your socks.

CHAPTER TEN

That Damned Village

MANAGING WORK RELATIONSHIPS

Q | A colleague of mine insists on using a comma before "while."

Q | Our new publications director insists on leaving in or adding unnecessary *thats*.

Q | A copy editor in my office insists on adding "of" after the word "all."

Q | I have a colleague who insists on using "as well as" at the beginning of a sentence.

Q | One of my colleagues insists on using the format 5th February, 2005.

"My boss/colleague/coworker/secretary insists on . . ." How many times have I read that opening line? Reading the mail, I wonder if there is a single office in America where colleagues get along. It seems to be an unfortunate fact that when people share writing tasks, there will be disagreement. And with disagreement, there is tension.

Almost any piece of prose that is subjected to copyediting is also subjected to scrutiny by others involved in the process of publishing it. Copy is passed from editor to writer and back again, then through project editors or managing editors on the way to typesetting. Designers may question content that affects the design; typesetters might question ambiguities in stylings or codes. Jacket copy or ad copy is routed past a dozen red pencils, and everyone has an opinion. Copy editors must negotiate with colleagues in order to protect the work of the writer on its way to the reader.

Even if you're freelancing at home, you will work with, and inevitably disagree with, an assigning editor. Glean what you can from this chapter, and be patient—the next chapter is especially for you.

In a workplace there is often a prevailing culture. If you're lucky, your coworkers are genial and collaborative and quick to give credit where it's due. When I was young, I worked at a magazine where the elderly assistant managing editor was always falling asleep at his desk. One of my coworkers was so concerned about embarrassing him during a nap, she would phone him and hang up before going to his office. (Historical note: This was in the days of huge, corded desk phones with jarring ring tones and no caller ID.)

I'm going to assume that this level of courtesy doesn't exist everywhere. Your coworkers may be competitive and ready to point fingers when there's trouble. Whatever your work environment, there are some commonsense guidelines to live by that I can pretty well guarantee you won't regret.

NO EDITOR IS AN ISLAND

If only you could do everything yourself.

Ha! Not only do we depend on our colleagues at work; we can't possibly do all the things they do, and often enough we don't have any real understanding of anyone else's work. It's easy to assume that delays caused by others are the result of incompetence or laziness. If you're the anxious type, such hangups can be stressful and irritating, and if you're not watchful, they can lead to accusations and arguments.

When it comes to laying blame for delays, that miraculous online schedule I described above does the finger-pointing in my office: since it publicly keeps track of and displays every stage of a book's progress, everyone can see where a project is languishing. It doesn't, however, always display the *reasons*. That can be a good thing if the reason you haven't finished editing Crankhauer is that you met someone cute at Gk2Gk, or annoying if the reason you're late sending out Purdy's page proofs is that the typesetters missed a chapter.

The point is, you can't always know why a colleague is holding things up. When glitches seem to be the fault of someone other than yourself, there's no need to get defensive or name names. Just send reminders and queries in order to notify others who are waiting for you to deliver. We've already covered the mechanics of using lists, schedules, and logs to keep track of who's on first. What's left is to focus on effective communication with others. I said my advice would be commonsense, so here it is: Play nicely, and work through channels.

Let's expand a bit.

PLAYING NICELY

There are approaches to office behavior that will stand you in good stead with your coworkers and grease the wheels of every negotiation, whether in spoken interactions or in written communications, specifically e-mailing.

Straight shooting in personal confrontations. When things are going well, it's easy to be cordial and cooperative in our dealings with colleagues. It's when there's trouble that we reveal our worst selves. (That same sweet colleague from the magazine who tiptoed around the narcoleptic assistant manager used to wake up the rest of us squabbling with the editor whose copy she had to fact-check. She remembers a time he confronted her at her desk while she was on the phone with a writer. While they yelled insults at each other, she could hear the writer through the phone whimpering, "Stop—please! Don't fight!")

So who hasn't flung an angry word or resorted to sarcasm in a tense office situation, or deflected blame to someone else behind his back, or resorted to manipulative tactics in order to get what we want? And does it ever help? Does it make us look good? A calm and fair statement of the problem, without exaggeration or finger-pointing, is more likely to enlist another's cooperation and reflect well on us. ("Linda, I'm worried about having the Henry project by October 1 in time for that conference. Do you think you can get it to me in the next day or two?")

I remember an incident at my first job when I flounced into the managing editor's office, slapped a piece of marked-up copy onto his desk, and said, "I'm sorry, but I can't work this way! Either Mrs. R. goes, or I go!" I was lucky he didn't call my bluff and hand me a pink slip right then and there. Instead, he burst out laughing, which made me laugh, too. But it's probably a rare tantrum that ends as well as that one did. On the contrary, such behavior not only makes us look bad; it tends to escalate a disagreement. In the same situation today, I would go to Mrs. R. herself and say, "I'd like to work with you in a better way. Can we talk?"

Like anger, negative attitudes add to office stress. So monitor yours. In a competitive environment, you can refuse to compete. If Tom receives praise or bonuses for productivity, reexamine your work habits and look for your own inefficiencies, with the goal to improve yourself, not to outdo Tom. In fact, you might ask him what his secret is. In a back-stabbing environment where others withhold information or show each other up in meetings, don't play that game. Be generous and open with your knowledge. Make sure you're up-to-date on everything before you represent a team, and give a private heads-up to a colleague who might be embarrassed by not knowing something you know. ("Barb, I'm making up the Jensen notes for the meeting, and my file says not all the art is in. Let me know if you have it now—then I won't have to mention it at the meeting.") Observe courtesies that cost you nothing. Watch yourself for little habits like frowning when someone drops work on your desk. You might just as well smile and thank him for the delivery, even if you both know you don't really mean it. Without being a Pollyanna about it, you can do your part to foster courtesy and collegiality in your workplace.

E-mail etiquette. Has anyone reading this not yet learned the hard way to take care when replying to "All," or when typing addresses (especially if your e-mail host automatically completes an address after you supply the first couple of letters)? We've all had misadventures in the minefield of e-mail: We've been misunderstood when we sent a brief and artless message. We've embarrassed ourselves with typos, crashed our recipients' computers with oversize attachments, and infected friends and loved ones with cyber diseases. That the potential for offense and personal humiliation through the misuse of e-mail is vast and terrifying is well known. But I can suggest some points of e-mail etiquette that will help you avoid misunderstanding, annoyance, and disgrace.

First, on forwarding messages: it's not polite to forward a colleague's message without asking, unless your established work arrangement with that person gives you implicit permission. Even then, you must be very careful. I was once dismayed when one of my coworkers forwarded our accumulated correspondence about a production issue to a consultant outside the company, forgetting that at the beginning of the correspondence I had written something graceless and impatient about that person ("Ovide wants such-and-such. What should I tell him?"). Another time, an acquiring editor forwarded my initial evaluation of a manuscript to the author. Those notes had been written for an in-house meeting for the purpose of estimating editing time; I had pointed out the clumsy word processing, the various cleanup chores the work would require, and a list of unresolved issues without any mention of the project's virtues. It was certainly not how I would have chosen to introduce myself to that author. Another courtesy when forwarding is to check first whether the recipient was copied in on the original message. One of my superiors regularly forwards e-mail to me that I've already received, which not only adds clutter to my in-box but also causes the occasional confusing déjà vu.

Second, it's impolitic to copy an e-mail to people other than the person you're nudging. Only under desperate circumstances should you do this, after you've tried more than once unsuccessfully to get a response from the person herself. It's especially mean to copy in the supervisor of the delinquent before she has a chance to explain what's going on. I can think of several times when I've been embarrassed or annoyed by the public airing of my alleged failings in group e-mails.

Even when the issue doesn't involve a problem, the inclusion of my boss in an e-mail to me on an innocuous topic suggests that the sender thinks I require supervision in the matter. One of my writers had a habit of copying the acquiring editor when he replied to my queries, and as a result I was reluctant to e-mail him at all. He didn't realize that I didn't necessarily want anyone else to read the kinds of things I was struggling with. I have a freelancer who always sends his bill to my boss, never mind that my boss then has to send it to me to copy and process and give back to her. The whole thing is almost funny when you think about it. But it still gets up my nose. Am I overly sensitive? Possibly—but if I am, no doubt others are, too, so take that into account when you go public with what might better remain a private exchange.

Third, be specific in your subject line; it's courteous to the recipient and an aid to finding the message later. It's anywhere from aggravating to alarming to receive a reply of "Yes—critical! Please do immediately" to a message you don't remember sending with a subject line of "IMPORTANT." You'd be in better shape if you'd written "Insertion for Hippely copy." If you recycle an old message from someone because it's easier to hit Reply than find their address, at least update the subject line.

And finally, set up your automatic signature to include full contact information. It's not always easy for your correspondent to locate the information elsewhere.

WORKING THROUGH CHANNELS, NOT OVER HEADS

Above, I gave the examples of asking Linda personally whether she could crank out the report on time and asking Mrs. R. for a talk about how to work better together. In both cases, the point was to address the person most responsible, and that person alone. In similar scenarios, however, I've been copied in on group e-mails like "FYI, Linda, the Henry project is now in danger of missing the conference date." No reasons are mentioned, but the damage is done—everyone thinks that Linda is responsible for the delay. Did the sender know that Linda received the final files only yesterday? Checking in personally with Linda before sending the note might have helped the sender phrase the note more diplomatically.

When paper copy circulates through an office and people make corrections and sign off on it, there's a special temptation to show up someone who corrects your work. A magazine editor friend of mine recalls the time she got back copy she'd edited from a superior who had "corrected" Aaron Copland's name, writing in the margin, "It's Copeland!!!" Incensed, my friend wrote, "It may be pronounced 'Copeland!!!' but it's spelled 'Copland,'" and rerouted it, humiliating the more senior editor. Although I have a feeling my friend still gets some evil pleasure from that memory, she herself admits that it wasn't politic.

"Working through channels" means playing by the rulebook rather than doing your own loose-cannon thing. But more particularly, it can mean solving a problem by starting with the person who's primarily responsible and not going over his head until all else fails.

Once, I received a poorly written index for an important rush book from a relatively new freelancer. Looking at the disaster, mental alarms sounded: (a) Bad indexer! (b) Delay! (c) Cover tail! I was out of my chair and halfway out the door on my way to the managing editor before I stopped and rethought. Instead, I took the index to the acquiring editor, who was familiar with the content of the book and was able to confirm my impression that it wouldn't do. Then I went back to my computer, reworked some of the pages with tracked changes, and e-mailed them to the freelancer, explaining the problem. I asked him to revise, and I told him of the urgency. A little while after sending the e-mail, I phoned him. The indexer had understood immediately, made some embarrassed apologies, and promised to fix everything as quickly as possible. Within twenty-four hours, he delivered an excellent revision.

In my mind, there were four beneficiaries of this tactic of addressing a problem at its root: I got my index, only one day late. The freelancer furthered his education. The managing editor had one less headache to tend to. And the reader gained an index that was truly useful. As a bonus, because the indexer demonstrated intelligence and cooperation in his quick and expert revision, I was happy to continue working with him, so the Press didn't lose a freelancer.

One last reminder: Working through channels entails e-mail etiquette as well. Giving thought before forwarding messages or copying people in can save your target some embarrassment and prevent trivial problems from escalating into personal vendettas.

EDITORIAL DISAGREEMENTS

At the top of this chapter, I gathered a bouquet of complaints that are surely familiar to anyone who edits as part of a group effort. Negotiating editing issues with colleagues is not really very different from negotiating with writers. The main differences are that (1) you share a style with your colleagues, and (2) you see them every day in the restroom (well, half of them anyway).

Because your style guide is an accepted arbitration tool in

your office, that should be your first stop on the way to resolving editorial differences. If you've made a decision to depart from style, you might have to persuade someone of the reasons. One of my colleagues once did so—the one whose author wanted to uppercase her job title on the book jacket. I lowercased it on the routing copy, and he e-mailed to plead his case. His message was a model of tact and flattery, all the way down to the smiley face at the end:

> Hi, Carol—I noticed that you, correctly, made the job title lowercase on the jacket. The author had requested that we capitalize her title and since it was part of a package of requests and complaints, most of which I wasn't able to accommodate, I figured it wouldn't hurt to let her have her way on this. I know it's wrong and I'm sure I argued with her about it during the catalog copy stage (and won), but would you mind if we eschewed Chicago style on this? If you do mind—and I respect that—I'll just pretend I didn't notice. Thanks. ☺

This made me wonder just how difficult this guy thinks I am, but he certainly made it easy for me to agree. (He could have saved us the exchange, however, if he had thought to scribble "Breaking style per AU request" in the margin.)

In cases of serious disagreement, look again at the strategies listed in chapter 4 for working with a writer: examine your motives for resisting; use tact in stating your case; let it go if it's a question of preference more than correctness; and as a last resort, appeal to a higher authority. And if the disagreement is with that higher authority? Assigning editors or bosses count as people and colleagues, too, only bigger and more powerful ones. Argue as much as the relationship will bear before you give in graciously. If you end up feeling forced to accept something that's flat-out wrong, file away some evidence of your efforts to correct it. And if that file begins to fatten, think about moving on.

TAKING RESPONSIBILITY

In an office atmosphere where your first instinct is to take cover when something goes wrong, you can help foster a more collaborative culture by owning up when you're the one who's responsible. People respond well to this. In their relief to be off the hook, they tend to be generous—they might offer reassurance or even share the blame. When you say "I'm sorry—I should have caught that," the response is likely to be "Well, we all should have caught it."

If you worry that people are blaming you for something that wasn't your fault, little good can come from laying blame elsewhere. If you think it's important to set the record straight, a low-key query to the person whose opinion you value most might be appropriate. ("I'm not sure exactly what happened here, but I'd like to know so it doesn't happen again. Could we figure it out when you have a minute?") Anger and defensiveness might deflect blame in the moment, but they won't enhance your reputation or ease future transactions with your colleagues.

If you have to work closely with someone who regularly causes trouble for you, try to take the high road, if you can, in order to get along. A friend of mine who was responsible for the final proofreading at a suburban Philadelphia newspaper in the 1970s remembers an eccentric composing-room foreman whose solution when copy didn't fit the page was to slice off the extra lines or paragraphs with his X-Acto knife and toss them in the trash. If the amputation happened in midsentence, he would stab in a period with a felt pen. My friend spent a lot of time rummaging in the waste bin to find out how the stories ended and then begging the guy to let her edit some sense into his results. True, there are a few reasons why this arrangement wasn't ideal. But she kept her job without costing him his, and the readers got mostly readable stories.[1]

COVERING YOUR TAIL

In spite of all your good-natured, together, supercollegial coping strategies, there may come a time when you're in the hot seat and you are forced to account for yourself. Maybe a big mistake cost major money. Maybe the company suffered a public humiliation. Maybe the photo of a society matron at the spring fund-raiser accidentally ran with the caption meant for the photo of a peacock spreading its plumes: "This old bird crawled out from behind a rock at the zoo to bask for a while in the warm spring sunlight." (A friend swears this happened at a newspaper where she worked.) When signs point to its being your fault, you will be asked to explain.

How aggressively you defend yourself is something you'll have to decide, but in order to have the choice, you have to have the means, and that's where your schedules, logs, lists, and folders come in handy. Somewhere in there is evidence that will allow you to reconstruct the timing and sequence of events, who notified whom, and what the exact instructions

---

1. In this book, my advice will be confined to editorial dustups. If a troublemaker at your workplace crosses the line into sexual harassment, bullying, or other inappropriate or dangerous behaviors, you may need a bigger book than this one, as well as help from your supervisor or human resources department.

were. And because of your habitual organizing of all that information, you'll be able to find everything you need.

But use it wisely. Control your impulse to e-mail the evidence to twenty people or march into the manager's office waving the printouts in triumph. If other people are stomping about demanding explanations, your ability to stay calm and rational may keep things from escalating. "I've looked at what happened, and I don't see how I could have done anything to prevent it. But if it was my fault, I'd like to understand how."

Of course, if your research shows that you screwed up big-time, it's also your decision whether to own up. I'm for it. "I made a big mistake" might not be easy to say, but if you don't have to say it very often, your reputation won't suffer, especially if you can follow up with a plan for making sure it never happens again. And write it down somewhere for your memoirs—everyone loves a good story about someone else's biggest mistake.[2]

KEEPING TRACK OF SUCCESS

I know I said we're not in it for the glory—but one of the nicest rewards of the copy editor's life is when a writer is grateful and bothers to say so in a public acknowledgment. You can bet someone in your workplace will hear about it if the author has problems with your editing. That's why, when you get positive

2. My biggest mistake? Twenty-five years ago, on the cover of a monograph I copyedited, the author's middle initial was wrong. I'll never forget the morning I came to work and found the acquiring editor (a skilled cartographer) trying to figure out a way to scrape off the initial and insert the correct one on the twenty copies we were sending to the author. Finally, sadly, he gave up. The author was a good sport about it. Even now, when I Google the book, I find "Image unavailable" in place of a cover photo.

feedback about your work, whether in print or in an e-mail, you should save a copy for your "brag file." Our managing editor reminds us regularly to pass along author compliments to her—she keeps a file that comes in handy when she wants to talk with her own boss about budgeting for promotions and raises. Many freelancers get permission from their clients to quote their tributes at their websites.

It's not immodest to promote yourself. If you are subjected to an annual performance review, you will probably be asked to make an accounting of your successes over the last year. So make a note of your achievements as they happen and add them to the file. If you brought in a difficult project on time, kept your projects within budget, edited an award-winning piece, worked well on a team effort, increased the amount of editing you were able to handle, took work-related classes, attended a conference—all these are worthy of mention at reckoning time.

A | Sometimes that's fine.
A | Sometimes that's fine.
A | Sometimes that's fine.
A | Sometimes that's fine.
A | He's wrong. Good luck.

CHAPTER ELEVEN

The Freelancer's Quandaries

Q | Can you tell how to became an editer?

WORKING FOR YOURSELF—WITH MANY BOSSES

Not all copy editors work in offices; many of you instead work on your own from home as independent contractors. Freelancing can be a terrific way of life, once you're up and running with reliable clients and a steady income. Not having to commute or punch a clock gives you the flexibility to be at home with children, travel, write novels, or to do just about anything else that would suffer in the 9-to-5 grind. There are obvious drawbacks, of course: no paid vacations or sick leave, no tech support, iffy health insurance. But my topic here is not to debate the pros and cons of freelancing: they're clear enough that in-house editors frequently talk about cutting loose, while freelancers daydream about salaried positions. Needless to say, freelancing is a huge industry that's valued both by editors themselves and by their employers.

Freelancers face most of the same issues that on-staff copy editors do. You have deadlines, overlapping projects, and writers with personalities. You use the same software, fight the same compulsions. You might even have to work with colleagues or employees, if your business has expanded beyond just yourself. But there are also differences, and they aren't trivial.

The most obvious difference is that freelancers are likely to be paid by several clients, which means that your record-keeping must be thorough and well organized in order to keep track of income and expenses. And if each of your clients has a different stylebook or set of procedures for preparing documents, it's up to you to keep track of the way they want things done—which dictionary they use, which style guide, the exceptions to the guide. Since another major difference of freelancing is that you compete with other freelancers for work, if you're high maintenance, you lose.

QUANDARY 1: WHEN IT RAINS AND POURS— ACCEPTING COMPETING PROJECTS

Freelancers don't usually set schedules and deadlines. An editor will phone or e-mail to ask about your availability, and she'll tell you the deadline and the number of hours of editing that's been estimated for the job. If she's desperate to find someone, and you aren't available or can't work enough hours per week to meet her deadline, she might change her schedule to accommodate yours. But if you need the work, and you don't detect desperation in her query, you might not be willing to risk losing the job by trying to negotiate. So here's your first quandary: you can either be honest and say you aren't free and lose the job, or you can say, "Sure—I'd love to do it," and lose sleep trying to deliver.

This is one way that even seasoned freelancers get themselves into trouble. Supervising editors are faced with the result of this all the time: the freelancer phones or e-mails to say that the edited copy will be late. A smart project editor pads her schedule to allow for some lateness, but that isn't always possible—and even when it is, it doesn't mean she won't be annoyed or remember your tardiness the next time she's hiring. It's better to be up front about your availability and productivity. Make yourself aware of the average number of hours per week you devote to editing, and don't be afraid to quote it to an inquiring editor to see if she can work her schedule around it. If you develop a reputation as slow but reliable, it will still be a good reputation. You won't be given certain rush jobs, but you'll be at the top of an editor's list for work that has a flexible schedule. (If you develop a reputation as someone who's talented but slow, you won't get the rush jobs, anyway.) There's room for a variety of work styles on an editor's freelancer list, but in her mind, reliability and good work will trump speed for any project where speed isn't an issue.

Although you might look at other freelancers as the competition, teaming up with one or two others whom you can recommend in a pinch can be a smart strategy for handling the occasional overflow of offers. A supervising editor will be grateful for the tip, and if all of you recommend each other for jobs, no one loses. Naturally, you must be certain that your teammates' skills are equal to your own before you recommend them.

QUANDARY 2: WHO TAKES THE HIT WHEN THE ESTIMATE GOES WRONG?

Experienced copy editors know the second quandary well: you've contracted for a project, and you're working along in it, and at some point the number of hours you estimated begins to look w-a-y too low. The possibility of tardiness is looming, and even if you're able to put in some overtime and meet your deadline, there's the question of whether it's wise for you to charge for many more hours than were estimated. You're on the honor system—there's no way your client will know whether you actually worked the number of hours you claim. You're thinking that if you put down the true number of hours you worked, you won't be believed; you'll be perceived as inflating your bill. The dilemma: either displease the client by charging more than she budgeted for the job, or short yourself, having worked a number of hours you won't get paid for.

I'm guessing that many more freelancers cheat themselves than cheat their employers when they face this choice. (One experienced freelancer tells me that she long ago gave up keeping track of her hours at all—she just bills the amount that was estimated.) But before you short yourself, consider carefully why the project took longer than estimated. Ask yourself the following two questions:

Question 1. Did the project involve a task that you hadn't met before and had to figure out how to do? When you're new at copyediting, there will be a learning period. Although it's not fair to make one employer pay for that, it is fair for an employer to tolerate a small part of your learning curve as an investment in future collaborations, in the same way they invest in new in-house editors. If the task was a basic, routine chore that you can expect to use in many future jobs, absorb the greater part of the cost of learning it yourself. If it was a bit tricky and not necessarily something you would expect to face again soon, split the difference and bill for half the extra time. If the task was something extraordinary that even a veteran editor would have had to puzzle out and that is unlikely to re-cur, bill the client for those hours, along with an explanation.

Question 2. Was the overtime really necessary, or was it the result of your slowness or compulsions? If you didn't know how to change the British punctuation to American with a few keystrokes and decided to change them all one by one, it's not fair for someone else to pay for what amounts to your igno-rance or poor judgment. You could have asked someone how to automate the task, and you could have checked with the su-pervising editor to find out whether it needed doing in the first place. Some chores that amount to cleanup can be done by the typesetter, and all you need to do is note them.

QUANDARY 3: WHEN THE PIPER WANTS PAY—
SETTING AND COLLECTING FEES

Perhaps the most vexing issue for freelancers is money. In-house editors take a paycheck for granted. On your own, however, it may seem as though you live with your hand out. What's more, you're constantly wondering whether you've asked for too little or too much. It reminds me of when I was fourteen and learned that all the other babysitters were getting a flat fee of five dollars for New Year's Eve. I knew I was under-paid at fifty cents an hour—that rate hadn't changed since my mother was in high school—and the family I worked for was constantly coming up short when it was time to pay. So when Mrs. Stubee inquired about New Year's Eve, I told her about the special rate. To my amazement, she agreed. But wouldn't you know—they left me with the children at six that evening and didn't come home until five in the morning. Eleven hours, and Mr. Stubee triumphantly paid me five dollars, not a penny more. Obviously, I've never gotten over it, although at least it taught me the concept of a minimum rate.

How much to charge. As a businessperson providing a service, it's your prerogative to set the rate and your client's obligation to inquire what it is. After that, all parties are entitled to negotiate. The trick is to learn what a reasonable wage is for (1) your level of experience, (2) the service you're offering, and (3) the employer you're working for. These are all separate concerns. After all, a beginning editor should not expect the same pay as an experienced one; a proofreader of fiction should not expect to earn as much as a copy editor of a technical manual; and you can't expect the same wage from a children's book publisher as you would get from a corporate legal department.

Finding your level will require a little homework. Do some research online at websites for freelancers like that of the Editorial Freelancers Association.[1] Or, if you're really stuck, you can ask your new employer straight out what she would normally pay someone in your position. You can say (if it's true), "I believe my experience puts me in the middle of your range." Ask for the top rate only if you're sure your résumé supports it (your employer will already know) and if you're confident you can deliver top-rate services. You might fear that letting someone else suggest a rate is a good way to get lowballed, but think of it merely as a starting point for negotiation. Most supervising editors will be fair—they want to find and keep good freelancers—but if based on your research (or your needs) the figure seems low, ask, "Could you manage [X dollars more]?" If the answer is no, you get to decide whether to accept the job. And don't assume that you are locked into a rate forever. As your experience grows, your client will value you more. At

---

1. Editorial Freelancers Association: http://www.the-efa.org/res/rates.php.

some point you will feel justified in asking, "Now that I've done X projects for you, would you be able to adjust my rate of pay?"

One of my colleagues who does freelance developmental editing in addition to copyediting stresses that although some jobs are worth more than others, a client won't necessarily realize that. She told me that she isn't shy about educating employers who don't understand the value of her services. If you're proofreading copy that wasn't well edited, send the client a sample edit and suggest that they let you copyedit for them next time.

Raking it in. Ideally, once your routines are established, collecting payment will take care of itself. At the start of a job, get something in writing in the form of a purchase order or a contract. If you work for someone who doesn't bother with such formalities and you're comfortable with that, at the very least you must keep a record of the agreement, and it's wise to send an e-mail confirming the terms before you begin, at least until you've established a working relationship with that person or institution. When you're just starting out in editorial freelancing, it's tempting to ask for partial payment up front. If the employer is an individual (as opposed to an institution) whose creditworthiness has yet to be proven, this might be a smart move, but otherwise it isn't customary. More common is the practice of sending a partial invoice when the work is partly finished, although this is usual only for projects that take more than a couple of months. It's fine to ask your employer about this.

When you're finished editing, you can either enclose an invoice with the completed work or wait for the client to acknowledge receipt of the work and satisfaction with it. But don't wait more than a couple of days. Prompt billing is essential to maintaining a steady income as a freelancer, and contrary to expectation, employers appreciate it: late invoices interfere with budgeting, and timely bills simplify their book-keeping.

Occasionally freelancers ask whether I will reimburse print-ing or postage costs, or if I could print out the editing myself and mail it to the author. These are issues that should be clari-fied at the start. Not many editing jobs involve actual printing out and mailing these days, so you can't assume that clients ex-pect to pay those expenses. There's also the nuisance of both-ering your manager with tasks she thought she had delegated to you. If you do incur expenses, hang on to receipts and log them in.

Finally, keep a careful log of your income. Once you earn over a set amount, the federal government will want to know about it. Since no one is withholding taxes from paychecks for you, you'll have to estimate your taxes and make quarterly pay-ments toward them.[2]

Dealing with deadbeats. Fortunately, most of the freelancers I know have little trouble with nonpayment. Many have expe-rienced delayed payments, however, so unless you have other ways to pay the mortgage, you'll have to stay on top of your accounts receivable. If thirty days pass with no response to an invoice, it's accepted business behavior to squeak your wheel: send an e-mail with a copy of the invoice and ask nicely whether the check is in the mail. Squeak as needed until you experience relief. In the rare event that all fails, you might have to threaten to take your complaint to a small claims court. That sounds drastic, but it's more polite and more legal than hiring a couple of burly guys.

2. Learn more at "Topic 554: Self-Employment Tax," http://www.irs .gov/taxtopics/tc554.html.

YOU'RE NOT ALONE

Although as a freelancer you might literally work at home alone, a community of fellow editors is as close as your keyboard or phone. When you have doubts or questions, reach out to the appropriate resource.

If you have an assigning or supervising editor, she is paid to monitor your progress and answer questions about what she wants. It's more helpful if you organize your queries into occasional batches than if you constantly bombard her, but you can be sure she would rather answer an e-mail from you now than sort out the mess later when the copy is on her desk. Feedback from supervisors is also an essential part of your education, so make it a habit to ask for it.

If you live in a city, there might be an organization through which freelancers share information and contacts. Getting involved with such a group will give you opportunities to talk shop, do some networking, and draw on the resources of others.

If you're stuck on a question about basic editing, do the homework yourself. If you can't find help in your style guide or dictionary, check online. Use electronic bookmarks to keep online reference works handy. For those times when you have all the information you need but can't seem to make a decision, join an electronic mailing list or forum of copy editors who help each other with editing problems. You'll be amazed at the community you find there—in fact, you'll wonder how anyone gets any work done hanging out at the cyber water cooler all the time.

More help with homework? Comin' right up.

A | Probably not.

CHAPTER TWELVE

Things We Haven't Learned Yet

KEEPING UP PROFESSIONALLY

Q | A number of my friends and colleagues now use *invite* as a noun, as in "send him an invite." I think it's pretty lazy usage when the perfectly good word *invitation* is available. Am I just an old crank who doesn't like change?

Consider this: people who haven't studied history or engineering or biology since high school or college naturally assume that their knowledge is outdated—that the subject has evolved and changed over time. They wouldn't dream of passing themselves off as professors or engineers or doctors. But even if the last time we studied English was in 1992, most of us somehow feel that whatever we learned about not beginning a sentence with *hopefully* or about *none* always being singular was the last word in grammar. Never mind that whoever taught us in 1992 was probably using grammar she learned in 1972, which very likely came out of a textbook published in 1952: we still believe in the rules of English we learned in our youth. Copy editors tend to be more confident of this than anyone. It's one reason we're copy editors.

I've lost count of the number of times I've been asked, "When did this rule change?"—as though there were a person or organization in charge of English, and rule changes were announced and could be identified by number and date. But there are no universal and immutable, God-given style and grammar rules. Language evolution is the ultimate in crowd-sourcing. Different voices, purposes, and levels of formality in writing allow for variance as well. Experts continue to write new grammar books, dictionaries, and style guides because the old ones continue to go out-of-date and because different kinds of writing require different guidelines. Sometimes rules solidify—especially grammar rules—because they serve well in most instances, but sometimes they're just rules because our teachers made believers of us.

Unfortunately, there are no college degrees in copyediting. Anyone who's noticed a delinquent apostrophe or two at the grocer's can hang out a shingle and—just like that—become a freelance copy editor. The best ones, perhaps, have been mentored in a job at a publishing house or newspaper. They began by proofreading and worked their way up to editing under the eye of an experienced editor who gave them feedback and instruction. But not everyone has an opportunity to learn in this way.

It can take years for a novice to get good at copyediting. Some have to learn the hard way: from angry writers whose work they've edited badly. In the meantime, they may make some smart corrections in the copy they read, but they miss other mistakes, and while they're at it, they *introduce* errors as well. They decide to spell out all the numbers but miss a few, causing inconsistency where there had been none. They replace a universally accepted jargon word that isn't in the dictionary with a more common word that alters the meaning of the sentence. They've never heard of the subjunctive, so they change it to the simple past. They needlessly contort a sentence to eliminate a passive construction. *They do harm.*

Language isn't the only thing changing over time: almost no one would deny that technology is a moving target. Just when you've mastered one version of Word or your e-mail or your phone, a new version is rolled out that flips everything around and offers new features, shortcuts, and confusions and wipes out all your customizing. But editors living in the technological past also do harm, lacking the proper tools for the job.

Now don't get all grumpy on me. Hating technology is a cliché. Technology cannot make you stupid or lonely or soulless (although I will grant that it can make you homicidal). And I'm not saying that you always have to have the latest version of everything; it's just that if editing is your job, it's reasonable for your primary tools to be up to standard for your editing assignments. You have to be able to send documents back and forth without weird conversions or loss of data—which means having a compatible version of whatever application your project is in, a high-speed Internet connection for research and communication, and the ability to manage and send large documents electronically, whether as scanned or compressed attachments or by uploading to a shared server or cloud folder. Knowledge of WordPress or more sophisticated content management systems is increasingly useful to editors, and essential for many. Being flexible enough to cater to a client's preferences adds value to your business. More to the point, what you need will continue to change. Ask your clients occasionally about the technology they are using. Now and then it's practical to resist the expense or bother of upgrading—but eventually if you don't refresh your equipment and skills, you will lose work.

In addition to these small-picture concerns, you would do well to keep an eye on what's happening in the larger world of publishing and publishing technologies, especially if you are trying to build a business or further your copyediting career. Knowing what short-run digital printing is, or print-on-demand, understanding the steps involved in self-publishing, following high-profile rights and royalties controversies, having at least a clue about who's buying what (newspapers, trade fiction, children's books, mass market) and in what form (hard copy or digital) will help you tailor your continuing education to the market. It will give you ideas on how to expand your services or retool to meet demands for new kinds of editing. It will allow you to converse intelligently with potential clients and employers or at conferences and workshops. It will prevent your being the last Luddite editor proudly waving your little red pencil while technology steamrollers on by.

If your skills are out-of-date, you will do harm in myriad ways. Take your pick: you can mess up the copy; anger and confuse the writer; embarrass your employer or client; distract, amuse, or shock readers; damage your reputation; lose work, sleep, and self-respect; and pretty much just ruin your life. But don't worry. There's no need for any of that to happen. After you've learned the fundamentals of editing and mastered its tools, you can stay current. The place to do that is online; that's where the information is. Luckily, almost all of it is easy to find and free, and it needn't disrupt your life except in one or two very good ways.

If you have a natural resistance to this type of learning—if you are at all tempted to skip the next two sections—please at least read the one called "Wait! Come Back!" and promise to give it some thought.

WEBSITES AND BLOGS

Many terrific websites offer free resources for copy editors: word-processing and editing tools (online dictionaries, style guides, thesauruses, acronym finders, macros) and tutorials (how to edit, how to proofread, how to use software), job listings, and more. A host of blogs and columns feature short posts and think pieces about usage and grammar by professional writers, editors, linguists, and other mavens; commenters (if invited) weigh in. Some content resides behind a paywall, but if you're able to go through a library, you can take advantage of their subscriptions. (Join your public library and check your alma mater to see whether alumni have online library privileges.) I've listed a few sites and blogs in "Further Reading." If you follow one or two and consider them worthwhile, they will lead you to others. In no time, you will find yourself taking part, whether you prefer to merely listen or join the conversation yourself.

SOCIAL MEDIA

If you haven't yet dipped your toe into the social media ocean, let me give you an overview of the types of resources on offer and what you might gain from each, along with a few caveats. But first, one fabulous reassurance: active participation is entirely optional. You can learn plenty just by looking on.

Twitter. A platform like Twitter can be just fun and scattershot, or you can configure it into a powerful learning and networking tool. This might surprise you. I remember the online chatter when the Modern Language Association posted its style for citing a tweet and the amount of backlash from commenters who were shocked at the idea of Twitter as a legitimate source of information for scholars.[1] I was dismayed by how many people still thought of tweeting as limited to the superficial (although perhaps understandably, given its chirpy terminology) and by how many not only chose to remain ignorant of the technology but were willing to boast of it in public. But would you sneer at someone who cites statistics from the website of a foundation or corporation? Or who quotes a political speech and cites a link to a video of the actual event? How is it any different if the same information is posted in a tweet? Well, for one thing, the reader of the tweet can access the original source with a single click. I can't dispute the fact that Twitter hosts a wasteland of inane blather; but it makes no sense to reject out of hand the original commentary and links to sources and data that also reside there. A limited Twitter feed that has been tailored to reflect one's own interests is a miraculously concise and efficient way to identify and aggregate a small selection of special-interest headlines from the daily avalanche of online news.

Using Twitter this way, you are more likely to connect with strangers than with friends. Relationships can be anonymous and need not be reciprocal: you can follow anyone with no need for their approval. And if you choose to follow mainly language writers and editors, the stream of tweets you see will contain advice and links to helpful articles about language and editing.[2] Dip in now and then to see what they're all talking

1. "How Do I Cite a Tweet?" MLA, accessed April 8, 2015, http://www
.mla.org/style/style_faq/mlastyle_cite_a_tweet.
2. In addition to following individuals, you can follow organizations, newspapers, websites, journals, and businesses, but remember that each of them is represented by a person or persons who write and post their tweets, which means that content and quality will vary.

about. One example: for a few days last year, a hot topic online was the discovery that the *Oxford Dictionary of English* lists "figuratively" as one of the meanings of *literally*. Skimming Twitter during that time, I saw many responses to this news: links to essays, links to the *Oxford Dictionary*'s own website, and short opinions and interpretations tweeted by writers and editors. I learned that most good dictionaries have listed this meaning for quite a while, but from outraged tweeters I saw confirmation of what I already knew: (1) that many people misunderstand the purpose of dictionaries, believing that the inclusion of a word or a meaning indicates "approval" of it, and (2) some people tweet kneejerk reactions without knowing the facts. It's a prime example of how spending ten minutes skimming through the tweets and posts can allow a person to gauge the progress of a particular controversy—and get a few laughs along the way (after all, why *wouldn't* I follow @TheOnion?).

Facebook. Whether or not Facebook is still hot when you're reading this, there will likely be a prevailing social platform whose main focus is family and friends, rather than strangers and professional contacts. Because of all the fun and personal posts and photos and videos showing up in your feed, this type of app is not the most efficient way to further your education in copyediting and technology. It is possible to set up a separate Facebook account that follows editing and publishing professionals in the way I described for Twitter, but because of the more personal nature of Facebook, you might end up learning a lot more about the families, vacations, and pets of those professionals than about their work.

Electronic mailing lists and discussion platforms. When we're working, it's common for a given style or construction to look wrong, and then look right, and then look wrong . . . and sometimes it's hard to look up the answer because we don't know the right grammar terms. Or we might be facing a tricky editing task that we don't know how to automate. That's where the online community of copy editors can help. On Facebook, Twitter, or at Copyediting-L or the Forum at *The Chicago Manual of Style Online*, a writer or editor can post a question and hope for good advice from peers. LinkedIn, a professional networking site, allows you to join groups based on special interests like editing, and some groups carry on active discussions. Even if you get conflicting answers, odds are they will help you better articulate the issue so you can do a more targeted search. And at least you won't feel alone.

WAIT! COME BACK!

This is the best part. There's no need to be checking in on all these blogs and social sites all the time, like homework. Rather, enjoy browsing when you have time, and give no thought to what you might have "missed." To keep track of your favorite websites and bloggers, put their addresses into an RSS feed (an *aggregator*) like Feedly or Netvibes, and take a look at the feed when it's convenient: you'll see a list of the sites that have updated since you last checked. Scan down the headlines and excerpts, and click through to any that look interesting. Often enough, there won't be much to look at—which is its own kind of reassurance that you probably aren't missing out on some huge language-trend scandal. With minimal effort you will know what language issues people are talking about, which ones they care about, and which ones are dismissed as unimportant. (You can always unfollow anyone who tweets six times an hour about what his cat is up to.) If you aren't careful, you might become a maven yourself.

Some people resist social media because they fear becoming "addicted." And I can't deny that on the forums and mailing lists I notice some people who seem to make a career of hanging out there. But I believe the risks are overstated. You are in control: if you don't want to be constantly checking your feeds, don't put the apps on your phone. If your excuse is that you aren't adept at computer tasks, well, you might have to fail a little in order to succeed, and I think it's worth a try. Though there may be some initial frustration registering at sites and getting accounts set up the way you want them, I suspect from my browsing that even people with below-average intelligence can figure these things out. You can do it. Consider it part of your job.

So take the classes and read the books. But if you want to continue growing and learning and loving your craft, you need to stay current—which means staying online.

A | The usage you frown on has been around for centuries, according to *Merriam-Webster's Collegiate Dictionary* (11th ed.). When a wording strikes you as strange or trendy, take a moment to investigate its credentials; even if you choose not to adopt the usage yourself, maybe it will help you be more accepting when others use it.

CHAPTER THIRTEEN

The Zen of Copyediting

Q | Contracts often employ defined terms in quotes and parentheses, e.g., ABC Corp. (the "Seller") shall sell ten widgets to XYZ Corp. (the "Buyer"). When drafting such a contract, I always put a period after the close parenthesis if it is the end of the sentence, such as in the above example. But it's like listening to nails on a chalkboard to me to have a period essentially (ignoring the parenthetical) follow the period employed in an abbreviation. What do you recommend?

THE X-TREME EDITOR

In a blog post listing the best jobs for people with obsessive-compulsive personality disorder, people with OCPD are described as "workaholics." "People with OCPD prefer working in a highly controlled environment, with rigid adherence to rules and regulations without any exceptions. This makes them ideally suited for jobs that require perfection, conscientiousness, and attention to detail, but misfits for jobs that require spontaneity, imagination, flexibility, or teamwork." Third on the list of jobs: copy editors.[1]

Hmm. . . . really? Sometimes I wonder. One freelancer I asked to do light editing returned a manuscript dripping with red, confessing that he "couldn't help it." The next time I hired him, he did it again. Both times, when sending his invoice, he mentioned that he had actually worked quite a few more hours than he was billing me for, and both times I felt that it was obvious why, so I didn't encourage him to bill for the whole amount. Not only was it awkward wondering whether he felt I was taking advantage of him, but I noticed on the second project that while he had been fiddling with all that rewriting, he had actually missed a few typos and misspellings.

Another editor, a colleague, admitted to me that before she learned how to change all the underlining in a document to italics, she highlighted each one and changed it by hand. She knew it wasn't necessary—that the typesetter would do it— but she did it anyway.

Of course I've already confessed my own little compulsion, in that endnote numbers scandal. And let's not even talk about my e-mail filing system.

When I use the word *compulsive*, I don't mean to suggest that copy editors literally suffer more than others from obsessive-compulsive disorder, which is an extreme and disabling illness. Rather, I'm talking about our propensity for meticulousness and perfectionism, traits that are important to us, and which in fact draw us to careers in editing in the first place. The problem is that there's no end to the amount of fussing you can do with a document, whereas there's a limit to

1. N. Nayab, "What Are the Career Choices for People with OCPD?," Health Guide Info.com, May 9, 2011, accessed December 18, 2015, http://www.healthguideinfo.com/living-with-ocd/p96632/.

the amount of money someone will pay you to do it. At some point it has to be good enough, and you have to stop.

WORKING TO RULE

It's common for an editing project to be assigned an estimated number of hours. At Chicago, we have various formulas for estimating, but we're aware that they're rough guides. It's difficult to guess what kinds of issues might slow the editing until we're well into the work. Regardless, experienced editors know that there are two kinds of projects: (1) the kind that deserves no more than the estimated number of hours, and (2) the kind that takes however long it takes. The problem is, how do you know which kind you're doing, and if it's type 1, how do you "work to rule"?

If you are a freelancer and you're offered a flat fee for a project, you can assume that the estimated number of hours is what you're expected to give it, and not much more. If you're being paid by the hour, it's usually easy enough to get a sense of a project's importance by asking the assigning editor. ("If I find that it's taking longer than estimated, is that okay?") Not that you'll get him to say that the job is low priority and the document doesn't need to be perfect. Rather, he will stress its importance if it's the kind of project that he's willing to invest more resources in. He might admit that the estimate was a rough one. He will always want to know if you run into difficulties with a project, but in some instances he'll be quicker to advise ignoring a time-consuming problem.

Working to a specified number of hours is a skill that develops with experience. When you start a project, divide the total number of estimated project hours by the number of working days before the deadline. This will tell you how many hours a day you are expected to put in. If you can't manage that many hours per day, perhaps because you are dividing your days among multiple projects, let the assigning editor know right away that the schedule isn't going to work for you. (And if you're a newbie, be conservative in guessing how many hours you'll last before falling face-first into the monitor—it might surprise you that few people can sit and edit eight hours a day.)

Next, figure out how many pages an hour you ought to be editing in order to finish in the specified number of hours. Here's how to do it. Start with the number of estimated hours. If the estimate includes cleanup, subtract about 15 percent to get the number of hours for editing. (Subtracting 15 percent is the same as multiplying by .85, if that's easier.) Next, divide the number of pages by the number of estimated project hours to see how many pages per hour you should be editing. You can then multiply the number of pages per hour by the number of hours per day to find out how many pages a day you should aim for.

Monitor your progress. After a few days, if you're on or ahead of target, fine. But if you're taking too long, make some adjustments. Figure out what's slowing you down and how you can economize. You might decide to live with a style that isn't perfectly in line with yours, if it's logical and consistent. (This might involve undoing some editing you've already done.) If you've been straying from spell-checking into fact-checking, dial it back. Sometimes checking facts is part of the job, but often we do it merely because we can't resist. Resist. If you've been writing long-winded queries or taking detailed style notes, try to labor less over them. If you've been going online to check the author's citations or find missing information, stop doing her job.[2] Query instead. Read faster. Look

2. Many editors take over authorial tasks to an unreasonable extent. When one of my colleagues finds a surfeit of mistakes in typeset proofs

again at my chapter 7: are you wasting time on tasks that you could automate, delegate, or reevaluate?

Non-editing tasks can also be big time-suckers. If you're juggling several projects at different stages of production, re-examine your habits and procedures to see where you can trim.

You might reasonably worry that making adjustments will entail lowering your standards. But let's not be silly. Some of our "standards" are just time-consuming habits that don't really make a difference to the reader. Letting go of them gives us time for more important tasks—and if working for our employers means working to a schedule, working for the reader means using the time we have in the best ways possible. So prepare yourself for the only extended use of italics for emphasis in this book: *The document does not have to be perfect.*

So how subversive is that? Not very. The document does not have to be perfect because perfect is rarely possible. There's no Platonic ideal for that document, one "correct" way for it to turn out, one perfect version hidden in the block of marble that it's your job to discover by endless chipping away. It simply has to be the best you can make it in the time you're given, free of obvious gaffes, rid of every error you can spot, rendered consistent in every way that the reader needs in order to understand and appreciate, and as close to your chosen style as is practical.

HANDLING STRESS BEFORE IT ESCALATES

If you're freaking out over the amount of work you have or deadlines that are piling up or a temporary inability to concen-

---

because the author has done a slapdash job or not actually proofread at all, she tells herself, "You can't care more about the book than the writer does," and stops herself from reading the proofs herself.

trate because of distractions in your personal life, identify the problem and do something about it. If it's a persistent problem, examine your habits and resolve to make some changes. If it's something more particular and immediate, you might have to ask for help in managing your work.

The solution might be to put in some extra hours. Or see a therapist, or get more sleep, or talk to a friend, or watch a funny movie. (My friend Sarah puts on the soundtrack of *Chitty Chitty Bang Bang*.) The important thing is to find a way to shine some light on the end of the tunnel.

You might be reluctant to confide in your manager that you need help, and it's not something you'll want to do very often, but in truly desperate times, a reasonable boss won't hold it against you if you end up whining a little or even falling apart. Some bosses are more tuned in to your state of being than others, which is bad if you'd rather not share, but good if you need the support. When I was experiencing a bad patch a few years ago, my boss e-mailed to say that I seemed "subdued" lately, or some such euphemism. I didn't think my work had been suffering, but I apologized in case it had. He wrote back that everything was fine but urged me to "take some time off if you need it" and reminded me that human resources was there to help. Exactly the appropriate response—supportive but not prying, and keeping professional boundaries intact. It moved me to take action to get myself back on track, although I wished at the time that I'd done it without prompting.

HAVE A LIFE

Put briefly, the way to bring your best to any job is to have a life away from the job. Good copy editors are liberally educated and culturally literate.[3] They know a foreign language or two, are reasonably numerate, and have traveled a bit. If you listen to music, read novels, raise pets or children or vegetables, rehab your house, or attend *Star Trek* conventions, I believe you'll be a better worker for it.

Ultimately, if you bring your best to your work knowing that the manuscript is not your life, you'll understand why one former colleague and mentor was not lowering her standards or abandoning responsibility when she used to counsel us: "Remember—it's only a book."

How deliciously subversive.

A | Yoga?

3. When I applied for my first job in academic publishing, at the University of Illinois Press, the test included having to identify a list of famous people. An editor there who was a friend of mine had once told me about the test, long before she knew I'd one day apply for that job. She had been embarrassed about not recognizing the name of one of the US presidents. I forgot all about it until I was taking the test and came to a name I didn't know—so I wrote that it was a US president. I hope it was. In any case, I got the job and sent flowers to my friend.

CHAPTER FOURTEEN

You *Still* Want to Be a Copy Editor?

BREAKING IN

It's a truism that to get a job that will give you experience, you need experience, and unfortunately editing jobs are no exception. With copyediting increasingly outsourced to freelancers, large in-house departments are becoming more rare, and the kind of apprenticeships we used to serve at the feet of a watchful veteran may not be as easily available, but it's still common for supervisors to mentor freelance editors with the aim of maintaining a stable of dependable employees.

Here at Chicago we are always looking for good freelancers, but for us to hire you, we require that you have experience copyediting scholarly content, and we ask candidates for in-house positions to take an editing test. Newspapers and magazines routinely follow the same drill.

So how do you get started?

One strategy, if you are young enough that your parents won't notice, is to move back home for a while and volunteer at a publishing company as an unpaid intern. When I worked in children's books, we had a series of interns, most of whom went on to find paid positions on the strength of their work for us and the recommendations we gave them. If you can't live at home, you might try to volunteer for a few hours a week, if your other job permits. As an intern, you can do certain chores, like coding, proofreading, evaluating unsolicited manuscripts, or updating e-files of edited copy, which will give you a feel for editing marks and an introduction to proofing and coding. Proofreading can be especially instructive if you are given the edited copy to proof against, since it will give you a chance to see and learn from the editor's corrections and queries. If you're smart and learn fast, your supervisor might be willing to recommend you for proofreading jobs elsewhere, which is a big step toward working as a copy editor.

Although many universities offer degrees in journalism, an alternative is a shorter-term course in publishing, like the one at Columbia University in New York City. A less expensive strategy is to take a class in manuscript editing. For instance, the University of Chicago offers a certificate through its Graham School of Continuing Education. There are also online courses. If you're a good student, the teacher can be a resource for finding job openings and might be willing to give you a recommendation when you finish the class. Many employers of copy editors require you to take a test, and an editing class will help prepare you for that.

If you can get work proofreading, you might be able to use that as a stepping-stone to work as a copy editor. If you happen to be knowledgeable in math or science or fluent in a foreign language, you might qualify for more specialized proofing or editing jobs, so be sure to mention it on your applications. If you get a nibble, the next step will probably be a proofreading test, so prepare yourself for that by learning proofreaders' marks and practicing on your friends' term papers and dissertations. *The Chicago Manual of Style* or another relevant style guide can be bedside reading at this stage. If you're able to say that you're already familiar with a particular style—such as

Chicago, or AP, or MLA—you'll look better to a hiring editor. Offer to do some trial proofreading at no charge. As a proofreader, you might be able to build a relationship with a supervising editor willing to ease you gradually into copyediting.

If you can find even just one job freelance copyediting, and then build on that to accumulate the experience of copyediting several projects for the same employer, it probably will not be difficult to parlay that experience into work for others. Many publishers require freelancers to pass an editing test before they will hire them, but at a certain point in your development, they may be willing to hire you on the basis of your experience and references. Many experienced freelancers have told me that word of mouth is their primary method of finding new clients.

Finally, there are countless print and electronic resources out there for you to explore. There are books filled with tips and resources; you can search for them online or in library databases or in person at your bookstore or library. The Internet is a mine of information for proofreaders and copy editors, whether you're trying to break in or already have years of experience. The "Further Reading" section of this book contains help for copy editors at all levels of experience.

I wish you well.

Further Reading

For an extensive bibliography of resources for writers and editors, I recommend the current edition of *The Chicago Manual of Style* (http://www.chicagomanualofstyle.org). For a short but valuable discussion of authoritative reference materials, including dictionaries, style and usage manuals, newsletters, and websites, take a look at Amy Einsohn's *The Copyeditor's Handbook: A Guide for Book Publishing and Corporate Communications*, 3rd ed. (Berkeley: University of California Press, 2011), 57–67.

What follows are just a few of the many excellent sources that can help you train as a proofreader or copy editor, further your education, and find work. If you skipped the section in chapter 12 called "Wait! Come Back!," read it now and pick a few of the following blogs and pages to put in your RSS feed.

PROFESSIONAL ORGANIZATIONS

The websites of professional organizations for editors offer members information about classes, editing tools and tutorials, job postings, national conferences, and local workshops and meetings. Even nonmembers will find plenty of advice and inspiration at their sites. In the United States, the American Copy Editors Society (http://www.copydesk.org) was founded primarily for copy editors in journalism, although in the last few years they have become more broadly inclusive of other kinds of publishing. The Editorial Freelancers Association (http://www.the-efa.org) is likewise a national, member-run organization with local chapters. Canadian and UK equivalents are the Editors' Association of Canada/Association Canadienne des Réviseurs (http://www.editors.ca) and the Society for Editors and Proofreaders (SfEP; www.sfep.org.uk). All are active on Facebook and Twitter.

BLOGS AND WEB PAGES

Katharine O'Moore-Klopf at KOK Edit (www.kokedit.com) blogs only occasionally, but her site is filled with links to online reference works and advice on getting started. Likewise, the Copyediting website (http://www.copyediting.com), operated by Erin Brenner, publisher, and Laura Poole, training director, is a trove of useful articles and links to courses, audio conferences, and job listings, although some of the content—such as the *Copyediting* newsletter—is for members only. Canadian editor Adrienne Montgomerie has a fun and resource-filled blog site called *Right Angels and Polo Bears: Adventures in Editing* (http://blog.catchthesun.net/) that includes her "Starter Kit for Editors" and podcasts you can download. Stan Carey blogs at *Sentence First* (https://stancarey.wordpress.com) and at the *Macmillan Dictionary* blog, and occasionally posts "Link Love," a list of links to recent grammar and language articles he found useful or entertaining. Ben Zimmer writes on language at the *Wall Street Journal*, Vocabulary.com, and elsewhere. John McIntyre's short but frequent antistickler posts on grammar and style at *You Don't Say* (www.baltimoresun.com/news/language-blog) are witty and educational. *Regret the Error* by Craig Silverman at Poynter (www.poynter.org/tag/regret-the-error) is a good site if you're interested in truth in journalism and how news organizations handle retractions. At Snopes (www.snopes.com), you can check the truth of rumors and urban legends. Editor and language writer Jan Freeman blogs occasionally at *Throw Grammar from the Train* (http://throwgrammarfromthetrain .blogspot.com/); and the tweets of lexicographer Erin McKean of Wordnik are well worth following (https://www.wordnik .com/; https://twitter.com/emckean). Mignon Fogarty's *Grammar Girl* blog is an excellent—and popular—source of grammar advice (www.quickanddirtytips.com/grammar-girl). You can follow all these writers and editors on Twitter.

Language Log (languagelog.ldc.upenn.edu) is a huge blog site with many bloggers, many of whom write technical linguistics posts that are over my head; but of those who also write regularly for a more general reader, I especially appreciate Geoffrey Pullum for his smart and hilarious rantings and Mark Liberman for his debunkings of popular language and science articles. Reading Liberman will make you more wary and analytical of what you read—less likely to believe (or worse, retweet) stuff like "There is no word for *father* in Mosuo" or "Use of personal pronouns is a sign of narcissism."[1] Pullum also writes more generally for the *Lingua Franca* blog at the website of

---

1. The categories in the *Language Log* sidebar are a treasure. Click on "Eggcorns," for instance, or "Crash Blossoms," and you'll get a whole roll of entertaining and educational posts.

The Chronicle of Higher Education (http://chronicle.com/blogs /linguafranca/), along with Anne Curzan, Lucy Ferriss, William Germano, Ben Yagoda, and other language experts.

There are many good online sources of answers to word-processing questions, but the ones I use most focus on help with Microsoft Word. I've already mentioned Jack Lyon's Editorium (http://www.editorium.com), which contains a mass of free tips and tutorials and tools (including one of my favorites, Advanced Find and Replace for Microsoft Word), as well as program add-ons you can try out before buying (such as FileCleaner and NoteStripper). The Word MVP Site (http:// word.mvps.org/) likewise has tips and tutorials on using MS Word for both PC and Mac and includes a troubleshooting section. Allen Wyatt's Word Tips site (http://wordribbon.tips .net/) is well organized to help you find quickly what you need to know for almost any version of Word. Finally, in addition to the "Chicago Style Q&A," the *Shop Talk* blog at *The Chicago Manual of Style Online* posts *CMOS*-related advice for editors and writers. You can follow all these writers and editors on Twitter.

NEWSLETTERS

Although the *Copyediting* newsletter is by subscription, it includes access to everything at the Copyediting website. Written by Erin Brenner and other top editors like Mark Allen, Adrienne Montgomerie, Katharine O'Moore-Klopf, Jonathon Owen, and Dawn McIlvain Stahl, the bimonthly newsletter contains news and features on grammar, style, and technology. *Editorium Update* (http://www.editorium.com/newsletr.htm), a free weekly e-mail newsletter written by Jack Lyon, is an excellent source of "tips about editing, writing, and typesetting in Microsoft Word." If you're curious about macros, the "Macros" category of the *Update* archive is a great place to start learning; Lyon takes you through clear explanations in baby steps. Allen Wyatt of Allen Wyatt's Word Tips also offers an excellent weekly e-mail of Microsoft Word tips free of charge.

FORUMS AND ELECTRONIC MAILING LISTS

Copyediting-L (http://www.copyediting-l.info/) is perhaps the largest and best-known electronic mailing list for copy editors. Hosted at Indiana University, it offers both list and digest subscriptions "for copy editors and other defenders of the English language who want to discuss anything related to editing: sticky style issues; philosophy of editing; newspaper, technical, and other specialized editing; reference books; client relations; Internet resources; electronic editing and software; freelance issues; and so on." There are two lists: one "where topics such as politics, religion, sex, and operating-system evangelism are forbidden," and an off-list chat where anything goes.

If an e-mail barrage is not for you, a more sedate community is the subscribers' Forum at *The Chicago Manual of Style Online* (http://www.chicagomanualofstyle.org/). There you can post an editing question and check later to see whether other users replied. (They usually do!)

Acknowledgments

Portions of the second edition are adapted with permission from my posts at the *Chronicle of Higher Education*'s *Lingua Franca* blog: "An Unexpected Truth about Copyeditors and Consistency," August 26, 2011; "Submitting a Manuscript? Leave the Typesetting to the Pros," September 6, 2011; "Before You Submit: Some Tips for Self-Editing," October 9, 2011; "Your Word Processor Wants to Please You," October 24, 2011; "What's So Hard about Reading a Cover Letter?," January 6, 2012; "Losing Is for Losers: It's Easier Than Ever to Back Up Your Work," February 3, 2012; "When Style and Grammar Rules Elude You," March 5, 2012; "Citing a Tweet: It's Not Just for Twits," March 23, 2012; and "Are You a Difficult Writer?," March 27, 2012. From the *Subversive Copy Editor* blog: "You've Got the Power: For Good or Evil," September 19, 2012; and "How Sticklers Give Copyediting a Bad Name," December 12, 2012. And from my essay "The Correctors," *Creative Nonfiction* 53 (Fall 2014): 16–17, with permission.

Sincere thanks to my many mentors and allies in editing, quite a few of whom could have written this book, and whose anecdotes and advice are at the heart of it: Mark Allen, Barbara Bagge, Alice Bennett, Erin Brenner, Rosina Busse, Mary

Caraway, Stan Carey, Erik Carlson, Leslie Cohen, Erin DeWitt, Jean Eckenfels, the late Amy Einsohn, Kelly Finefrock-Creed, Kate Frentzel, Jenni Fry, Mary Gehl, Ruth Goring, Teresa Hagan, Russell David Harper, Sandra Hazel, Susan Karani, Leslie Keros, Michael Koplow, Heidi Landecker, Caterina MacLean, Margaret Mahan, John E. McIntyre, Mara Naselli, Susan Olin, Mark Reschke, the late Claudia Rex, Maia Rigas, Anita Samen, Christine Schwab, Joel Score, Edward Scott, Rhonda Smith, Cheryl Solimini, Rebecca Sullivan, Ruth E. Thaler-Carter, Nancy Watkins, the late Lila Weinberg, Lys Ann Weiss, Laura Westlund, and Yvonne Zipter.

For professional advice and enthusiasm, I am grateful to Laura Andersen, Rossen Angelov, Marc Aronson, Victoria Baker, Tristan Bates, Kira Bennett, Susan Bielstein, Nathan Bierma, Dean Blobaum, Michael Brehm, Perry Cartwright, Joe Claude, Joan Davies, Lindsay Dawson, Paula Barker Duffy, Joëlle Dujardin, Will Dunne, Elizabeth Fama, Lucy Ferriss, Eric Gamazon, Clifford Garstang, William Germano, Alister Gibson, Ellen Gibson, Kate Hannigan, Kathleen Hansell, Mark Heineke, Rob Hunt, Jaci Hydock, Brad Inwood, Penny Kaiserlian, Blair Kamin, Carol Kasper, Garrett Kiely, Linda Hoffman Kimball, Mary Laur, Charles Lipson, Robert Lynch, Sylvia Mendoza, Jane Miller, Sarah Oaks, Gregory Opelka, Joseph Parsons, Joseph Peterson, Randy Petilos, Rodney Powell, Geoffrey Pullum, the late Chris Rhodes, Lauren Salas, Jill Shimabukuro, Logan Ryan Smith, Inés ter Horst, Margie Towery, John Tryneski, Joseph Weintraub, Ben Yagoda, Aiping Zhang, and Sara Zimmerman.

I am indebted to Mark Allen, Kathy Dorman, Elizabeth Fama, Russell Harper, Tiana Pyer-Pereira, John Saller, Ed Scott, and three anonymous reviewers for the Press, all of whom read drafts and offered suggestions for improvement and expansion. I am especially grateful to Marilyn Schwartz for her many wise and inspired suggestions. Erin DeWitt, Mara Naselli, Ed Scott, and Lys Ann Weiss gave me special help with the chapter on freelancing. Russell Harper has an extra claim to thanks for taking over the editing of *The Chicago Manual of Style Online Q&A* in January 2001 and maintaining it with expertise and hilarity for nearly three years. Thanks also to Ruth Goring for her endless tact and good humor as my go-to grammar mentor, and to Ruth, Russell, Anita Samen, and Kelly Finefrock-Creed for years of continuing collaboration on the "Chicago Style Q&A."

At the University of Chicago Press, my editor, Paul Schellinger, listened to, challenged, and tactfully prodded me into shaping and finishing the book. David Morrow handled the second edition with amiable counsel and great patience. I am indebted to managing editor Anita Samen for her tolerance, sense of humor, and feisty and effective management style, and to Carol Kasper and Ellen Gibson, whose open-minded enthusiasm has launched my work in rewarding new directions. Erin DeWitt's expert and generous editing twice improved the book in countless ways; she has my warmest thanks. Having both Christine Gever and Gregg Opelka as proofreaders kept me serene in the final stages of production. Sincere thanks, too, to Isaac Tobin and Joe Claude, who respectively designed and produced these elegant pages, and to both Ellen Gibson and Lauren Salas for their kindness, generosity, and marketing savvy.

To my sons, John and Ben, I dedicate this book with love and gratitude.

Index